"When I hear Brittany teach, when I read her words, I want to keep moving. I want to get going. I want to stand up, live boldly, and not quit. This generation needs her words and her leadership, in Jesus' name."

—**Jess Connolly,** author of *You Are the Girl for the Job*, founder of Go + Tell Gals

"Brittany is the best friend every girl has longed for. Her way with words in *Flip the Script* will bring you to tears and challenge you but also inspire and encourage you to see the true beauty God created you specifically to be."

—**Danielle Busby,** star of TLC's *OutDaughtered*

"Huge congrats on the book! What an accomplishment! I'm looking forward to seeing it on shelves."

—**Bob Goff,** *New York Times* best-selling author of *Love Does*

"In a world where women are overwhelmed with the weight of comparison, jealousy, and unmet expectations, Brittany invites us to reframe the way we see and know God, ultimately finding our identity and worth in him. This book is a must-read for all who are looking for revival in their faith, commissioning them to live with their new mindset of courage and confidence in Christ."

—**Alexandra Hoover,** best-selling author of *Eyes Up*, ministry leader

"Whether we recognize it or not, we are all storytellers. We tell ourselves stories about why people stay and why people leave; about what makes us significant and what keeps us safe in the world. The brilliance of this book is that it calls out the common narratives that are dampening our joy and hindering our growth, and it empowers us to write a new story—a story of truth that leads to peace. If you're ready to start flipping the script on some unhelpful narratives in your life, this book is for you!"

—**Nicole Zasowski,** Marriage and Family Therapist, author of *What If It's Wonderful?*

"*Flip the Script* is a powerful message that will change the way you think about God, yourself, and others forever. If you have ever struggled with negative self-talk or debilitating narratives that paralyze you from moving forward, Brittany's words are a salve to those wounds. She calls out our lies and replaces them with tangible tools of truth. Brittany's honest reflections will make you pause and examine the thoughts that have been holding you back and give you permission to take them before the Lord and find freedom in Scripture."

—**Bailey T. Hurley,** author of *Together Is a Beautiful Place*

"Infused with hard-won wisdom, this book will take you on a journey to live the life you were created to live! Brittany has a flair for life that shines through her message, and if you desire to be the best you that you can be, this is the book for you! Come flip your script and step into brilliance!"

—**Kara-Kae James,** Mom Up

"In a time when it is easy to be overwhelmed with all the bad, and happiness just seems to be a moving target, Brittany offers a better option. With practical steps and God's truth, she teaches us how to embrace joy and hope."

—**Simi John,** speaker, author of *I Am Not*

"We all have broken scripts. They hold us back and prevent us from living fully in the truth of who we are in Christ. Brittany beautifully bridges the gap from broken to beautiful and helps us recognize areas where we need to bring our thought lives back into alignment with Scripture. Pick up this book if you want to be guided into a journey of living freer and less hindered by the lies we often believe about ourselves."

—**Rebecca George,** author of *Do the Thing*, host of the *Radical Radiance*® podcast

"How often do we carry the weight of our shame with us everywhere we go? It continues to weigh us down as we move from relationship to relationship. Brittany does a beautiful job of helping us release shame, doubt, and identities the world has placed on us and run with open arms back into the presence of Jesus, allowing him to lift those burdens off us."

—**Alissa Circle,** Founder of Be Together Co, author of *(Be) Known*

"Brittany provides a real and raw look at her own struggles while beautifully showing the truth from God's Word that has set her free. It is only when we embrace who God is and what he has done that we begin to walk in the freedom he provides. This book will touch your heart. You will be challenged, comforted, and encouraged."

—**Jeremy Freeman,** pastor, speaker, author of *#butGod*

"*Flip the Script* is a message for such a time as this! It's important for upcoming generations to know their worth so they can walk in their purpose. If the devil can keep them feeling like failures, they'll never be able to walk in victory and true freedom. This book gives biblical and applicable ways to flip the script on the enemy's tactics and allow God to mold and shine brighter than ever."

—**Andrea P. Bourgeois,** author of *Just Breathe* and *Anchor My Soul*

Flip the Script

Make Your Move from Broken to Brilliant

BRITTANY ESTES

LEAFWOOD
PUBLISHERS
an imprint of Abilene Christian University Press

FLIP THE SCRIPT

Make Your Move from Broken to Brilliant

LEAFWOOD
P U B L I S H E R S
an imprint of Abilene Christian University Press

Copyright © 2023 by Brittany Estes

ISBN 978-1-68426-162-8

Printed in the United States of America

Published in association with Books & Such Literary Management, 52 Mission Circle, Suite 122, PMB 170, Santa Rosa, CA 95409-5370.

Cataloging-in-Publication Data is on file at the Library of Congress, Washington, DC.

Leafwood Publishers is an imprint of Abilene Christian University Press
ACU Box 29138
Abilene, Texas 79699

1-877-816-4455
www.leafwoodpublishers.com

23 24 25 26 27 28 29 / 7 6 5 4 3

Contents

To Rachel and Kenzie—you are the reason this book exists. You are the faces I pictured as I wrote these words. You are why I want to spend my days fighting for this generation. Thank you.

To my children—those who are officially a part of the Estes fam and those who have lovingly been called 8, 9, 10, and so on—if you get nothing else from these pages, know that I am honored to be on this journey with you. I will fight for you when you have nothing left in you. I will champion you into seeking God's best. And mostly, I want you to see that being sold out to Jesus is not a weak or lackluster life. It's the greatest thing you can ever do and the wildest ride of your life.

FOREWORD

Like my friend Brittany, I'm a runner and mom. And for the most part, I need music to run.

Of course, I love the occasional silent mile, but I usually find songs that carry a tempo I can time my footsteps to. And every once in a while, the perfect song comes along, in that it will help me keep the best pace for my body.

A few years ago, I found my perfect pace song: "Pompeii" by the band Bastille. It's got a great build, incredible tempo, and it sounds somewhat upbeat.

But after a handful of long runs listening to "Pompeii," I realized the words were all wrong—at least for someone like me. For example, some of the lyrics pose the question: "How am I going to be an optimist about this?" And later in the song, the singer asks: "Does it almost feel like nothing's changed at all?"

Nothing makes me feel more like a mom than when I nag my kids about what kind of music they're listening to. One minute I'm feeling young and free, and the next, I'm poking a teenager repeatedly, asking, "But what do these lyrics *mean* to you? What do you like about this song?!"

I remember being an adolescent myself—it was not too long ago (right?!). I remember caring more about a beat than I did a lyric. There was no overthinking what listening to a particular song said about my soul. But I can't help talking to my children about it now because I know that the song we sing matters.

When it came down to it, I had to delete "Pompeii" from my running playlist. The defeat that lives just under the surface of my soul can't handle such subtle messages of discouragement. Because the song we sing matters.

I don't know a single woman who doesn't need help flipping the script—not one.

I'm so grateful for my friend Brittany because she's going to help us hear the song we're singing and replace it with truth. As you're about to find out, Brittany is the girl for this job because she's had to change her song as well. She's been through the struggles of uncertainty and defeat, so she understands the work we are embarking on. If you're ready to step out of discouragement and into truth and triumph, you've come to the right place.

Your life, your days, your runs, your family, and your soul are far too important to keep speaking or singing defeat.

It's time to flip the script, amen?

Jess Connolly
Author of *You Are the Girl for the Job* and founder of Go + Tell Gals

The Scripts
THAT DERAIL US

There are two kinds of people in this world: those who live for fair rides and those who loathe them. You cannot be anywhere in between. Trust me, this is so.

Growing up, I couldn't wait for the week our town would proudly host our county fair. The bright lights, farm animals, rides, and funnel cakes were all a dream. When fall rolled around during my senior year of high school, it was no surprise that I was excited to go. That year, my parents let my sister and I go with two guy friends we knew from church, unchaperoned. Man, it felt great to be so grown up.

We had the best time with our little group, laughing, eating all the food, and going on the rides. It's funny how when you're a kid, you don't question whether those rides are put together well as you climb into the seat of each one; you just assume the best and jump on in. It's probably the same sort of logic that allowed me to ride the infamous Gravitron, followed by the spinning teacups. About five seconds into the spinning teacups, I realized the mistake I had made—not just the obvious one of hopping on a questionable ride, but the "eating all of the fair food prior" one as well. I felt as though my life were flashing before my eyes with each spin. The laughter of my friends and sister echoed in my ears as I desperately tried to focus on one spot so as not to spew my "excitement" and deep-fried goodies all over everyone. *How did I get to this point? Why didn't I see it coming? We have to stop this spinning madness.*

As the ride (also known as my torture chamber) came to a stop, the operator signaled that we could leave. With a sense of urgency, I darted out of my seat and located the nearest trash can. Nothing had ever appeared more beautiful, and green. It was there, while heaving over a smelly bin in the middle of all the chaos, that I decided I was no longer a fan of the good ol' fair and her fancy rides. No, she had done me wrong, and our breakup was both swift and painful.

Our World Is Spinning

Years later, I was met with the same churning feeling I had once known on those teacups, but this time, it felt worse. I didn't think anything could make me feel that sick again. It wasn't a silly ride, and I certainly didn't know how to make it stop. A few days prior, I watched as two girls, both of whom I had heavily invested in and loved dearly, just snapped—one with a public nervous breakdown, and the other with a foiled attempt at ending her own life. I didn't understand what happened. On the outside, these girls seemed to be thriving and enjoying life. Did they have struggles? Sure. But nothing that I thought would ever lead to hospitalization and life-threatening moments. I couldn't get their faces out of my mind, and that morning, I woke up with a sickening feeling. The room was spinning, and I thought I might vomit, as years of work and conversations with women finally coalesced into one huge realization. My eyes opened to a generation of drowning young women who searched for worth, validation, truth, and purpose. Many even questioned their existence. I had been having many of these same conversations, over and over again. That experience taught me that this is the result if those thoughts go unchecked.

Bright, beautiful women were drowning at alarming rates. They were lost in a world where they could never measure up. But that wasn't all—nobody seemed to be rescuing them.

So here I am, your new pink-haired bestie, ready to tackle this mess with you.

I'm well acquainted with your struggles. They were mine, too.

What if there is another way? What if your life doesn't have to be defined by what others say? Or even what you say to yourself over and over again? Or what social media mandates? What if I told you that beauty and life are yours to be found, all while being exactly who God created you to be? What if you knew that freedom beckons you?

Freedom is possible. There is more for you, so much more. I hope you find hope in this book. I hope you mark up its pages, spill your coffee on it, and wear it flat out, because once we're done with this book, you won't question how incredibly remarkable you are. Why? Because you'll learn something that will change the trajectory of your life. The truth is tucked in 2 Corinthians 10:5. It's simple but life changing. The apostle Paul wrote, "We demolish arguments and every pretension that sets itself up against the knowledge of God, and we take captive every thought to make it obedient to Christ" (NIV). The problem you've been facing? It is nothing but bad scripts containing negative, broken, lie-filled sentences that you hear in your head as you work, play, and go about your life. These scripts are side-lining you, maligning you, and harming you. But they need not mess with you any longer. You will learn how to "take captive every thought" by flipping those internal scripts. I will show you how.

It's time to silence all the voices so you can hear the One who really matters. Whether you feel it or not, there is so much noise in your own head as you grapple with who you are, where you're going, and what you're worth. These negative scripts represent a lie, a distraction from the evil one. He can be so sneaky and persistent that he can have you wrapped up all in yourself that you can't even see what's going on. You just feel lost, paralyzed, and defeated. But one thing is clear: Satan is predictable, and I have his number. Jesus reminds us in John 8:44: "He was a murderer from the beginning, not holding to the truth, for there is no truth in him. When he lies, he speaks his native language, for he is a liar and the father of lies" (NIV).

Here is how we win. We're going to highlight some scripts that have broken you down, that have possibly flat-out shattered you. The great news is that you are never broken beyond repair. In fact, I want to show you how God plans to gently collect all your pieces and put them back together as you retrain your mind to think differently about your situation, God, and your world. Once you've learned how to flip your old script in a way that represents the truth of Scripture, you will emerge stronger than before. These are real-life script flips you can create to be made whole again. However, this journey is not easy or quick. Flipping negative scripts will take time and lots of work on your part. But you won't be doing it alone. I'm right here with you, screaming for you like a schoolgirl on the Gravitron.

There will be freedom, trust me. I can speak to it because I've experienced it, not only in my life, but in the lives of many other women. But I don't want us to stop there; I need us to look around and see the women all around who need us. They are counting on you to do this hard work of restoration so you can lead them through it as well. Sister, your freedom will be contagious to them. I can't do it alone; I need you, too!

Are you ready?

Let's discover your negative scripts and truly flip them.

CHAPTER 1

Old Script:
I AM A FAILURE

I'm good at failing. Some people have a long list of wins and accomplishments. I, however, have a long list of failures. It's funny, even though it's not. Let me explain.

In high school, I had a slight addiction . . . to tanning beds. Yes, I know now how silly that was, and I know all about the harm tanning beds can cause your body. But as a high school sophomore, I believed firmly in my invincibility. This pasty white girl wanted a golden bronze color. So bring on the ultraviolet bed! I will say, though, that I was a stickler for wearing my goggles when I tanned. The worker at the tanning salon cautioned me about the effects of not wearing goggles and what it could do to my eyesight. This sister didn't need to be told twice; I wore goggles every time. Nothing could mess with my perfect twenty-twenty vision. Because of the goggles, I had amazing orange and white raccoon eyes.

Each day after school, I'd drive to the tanning salon and bake for twenty minutes. Shoot, even before I could drive, my grandma would take me after I got home off the bus. She'd drive me there and sit in the car smoking a cigarette while I went inside. (Yeah, Grandma was a character.) Oh, how I looked forward to those twenty minutes every day. Most of the time, I'd turn on the fan in my room, blast the music, and take a short little nap. It was heaven. But one afternoon, things didn't go like they normally did. At some point in my heated nap session, my goggles slipped off my face, and my pasty white eyelids no longer boasted white. Nope, they became like crusty lobsters.

High school is tough, friends, even in normal circumstances. But when your eyes are crusted and swollen and you're unable to wear makeup—that's just tragic. Or at least it felt that way to me. *Why did my parents make me go to school looking like this? Did they hate me?* Somehow, I persuaded the school administration to allow me to wear sunglasses until my eyelids healed. I think they just didn't want to hear me whine any longer. Either way, I sported my sassy 1950s-inspired leopard-print sunglasses for days. The situation went from being the worst to the coolest.

During my sunglasses phase, we learned a new concept in geometry class. My teacher shut the lights off in the class as we followed along with her work on the projector. This dates me a bit—hello, 2001! But with the room dark and my sunglasses providing even more shade, I quickly fell asleep. In my mind, I still play out that day as if I were incognito and nobody even knew I slept. But who was I kidding? Everyone must've known. I was the ridiculous girl wearing sunglasses in the dark with her head on the desk, probably snoring. No secrecy. No mystery. That's when I missed the news about this particular geometric information: what we were just learning would appear on our semester test, a test that if we were to fail, we would be forced to take the class again.

Did I study for the test? No. I felt invincible, aside from the crusty eyes. I always had. I could go in and take that test and pass with flying colors. Not this time. I didn't just fail; I failed miserably. There I sat, in a group of class clowns, troublemakers, and other slacker kids pulled into a special class to retake the semester. It was so embarrassing and all my fault. Lack of effort and conviction proved to be my demise. Hidden behind my sunglasses, I chose to nap and not pay attention, and because of that, I faced the consequences.

The whole story is a joke in my family. "Brittany's so good in math that she took geometry *twice*." Or, "You would know, you took the class twice!" Cue the laughter. It's all said in jest and, shoot, sometimes I'm the one leading the charge. But if I'm honest with you, that script stings. Those words have found a place inside and have changed the way I see things. My goals, dreams, and abilities are now filtered through the lens of failure. The script plays like a broken record. *You can't do this; you're too lazy. Remember that one time you failed here? That's all you're good at.* More times than I'd like to admit, I believe the script as truth. I accept defeat before I even try, all because of a careless sentence thrown my way. "The tongue has the power of life and death, and those who love it will eat its fruit" (Prov. 18:21 NIV).

It doesn't have to be a dramatic or devastating event, but that seed of failure can be planted at any moment. Without warning, it will grow into a giant tree, becoming a barricade between you and your future, blocking your view of any possibilities, and keeping you hidden in its shade. That's the power of a negative script.

Jenny knew what I talked about. The pain of failure ripped her in two every time she saw a mother with a newborn baby. She desperately wanted a baby, but she struggled to make it a reality. She trusted me, and while we sat outside of a coffee shop, her hands gripping her cup, Jenny opened up. She shared with me the pains of her infertility journey and how she had conceived a handful of times but that each one had ended in miscarriage. Her body didn't cooperate, and because of this, Jenny labeled herself a failure. "I'm just a failure, and I think God is punishing me," she said.

"Wait, what? You are not a failure. And why do you think God is punishing you?"

That's when she couldn't hold it in any longer: "I've never talked about this to anyone before." While in college, Jenny fell in love with a boy in her literature class. About a year into dating, she found herself pregnant. Growing up in a Christian home, Jenny thought she couldn't go home and tell her parents that she had messed up. So she felt she only had one choice. Jenny and her boyfriend scheduled an appointment at a local abortion clinic.

On the day of her appointment, Jenny's boyfriend drove her to the facility because her emotions and anxiety overcame her. But he could only stay in the waiting room while she ventured into the back of the clinic by herself. Her heart raced and her body shook with each step down the hallway. The room appeared dark, sterile, and cold. Trying to act like a grown woman, choking back tears, and feeling full of fear, she just wanted her mother. But the person she needed couldn't know this moment ever existed. She had gotten herself into this mess and would need to get herself out of it—on her own.

The procedure (as they called it) happened quickly. The pain came in waves, and it was nothing she ever dreamed of. She felt dirty, shameful, and completely exposed. Though the physical reminders of what she endured only lasted a short time, the emotional and mental scars have stayed with her to this day— her dirty little secret.

But years later, as she tried to have children, she questioned if she struggled due to God punishing her for her abortion. Had she not made that choice as a college student, then she wouldn't be struggling now, she thought. She felt that she had failed so greatly, her life would never be the same.

It's funny how these scripts play over and over in your head and embed themselves into your heart without permission. I'm no stranger to that feeling. For me, these phrases echo like a parrot who's eager to chant the new words he's learned: *You're a mess; you're a mess. This is your fault; this is your fault. You can't do anything right; you can't do anything right.*

It's the small, simple scripts that stick the longest. They're sneaky like that, and the longer they have the freedom to run your heart and mind, the harder they are to correct. Because they are short and insidious, you don't even realize there's a problem until you see how they've spread through your entire life and have caused you to question every choice, mistake, or direction; to wonder if current struggles are a reflection on past failings, God's punishments, or your entire worth. You start to believe that life would be easier if you were good enough, if you made all the right choices, if you never let people down. Can you relate? I would bet that I'm not alone in these thoughts. Remember, I'm good at failing. We forget this simple statement: "There is no one righteous, not even one" (Rom. 3:10 NIV).

A few years back, I found myself on a stage while helping host a children's ministry event with my husband, Sam. That particular night, the church filled with people of all ages. It was such a fun sight to behold. At the end of the event, we brought up our favorite dancing third-grader, and I challenged him to a dance-off. My plan was to make the crowd laugh; I'm pretty good at that, so that wouldn't prove too hard. That's when our little third-grade buddy started to breakdance. *Say what? It's fine, I'm fine, everything's fine. This kid is going down*, I thought. He busted a few moves that I couldn't name even if I tried, so I answered back with some hilarious attempts of my own. That's when I decided to get serious. After his next series of ridiculously skilled stunts, I dropped down trying to land a one-handed handstand trick. The crowd would jump to their feet in an uproar while cheering me on, because who doesn't get excited seeing a thirty-year-old woman breakdance? But things didn't go as planned. When I tried to stick the move, my hand gave out, and I collapsed onto the floor. Somewhere between the adrenaline rush of excitement and the horror of the fall, I heard a pop. *Shoot. This can't be good.* But as a trained theater actor, I hopped up, shook my hand, and continued on with the show. The reality hit the moment I stepped off the stage. My thumb throbbed.

After a few days of denial, a crazy hand X-ray in a veterinary clinic (that's a story for another day), and a giant black-and-blue hand, we realized that this might be a big deal. A trip to the orthopedist confirmed that it was worse than we imagined. Not only did I break my thumb, but a piece of bone that was attached to the muscle became detached, and I had another tear straight down the top of my thumb. All of that would result in a surgery, a gnarly scar, three casts, and four months of rehab. Still to this day, I struggle to open containers or grip things with that thumb for extended periods of time.

Every time people ask what happened to me, I laugh and say that I broke my thumb while breakdancing. Because obviously that's the answer you expect from a sane, grown adult. What an unexpected story: the time I failed and did so massively in front of a large crowd of people.

The pain of failure is real and, in my case, costly. Often, that negative script causes me to pause for fear of failing all over again. Who wants to take chances when the cost of failing can be so great? Maybe that's why we've stopped taking risks, moving forward, and contemplating our purpose.

In my time coaching women, there seems to be one big common obstacle they face: the fear of failure. Recently, I put out a poll on social media to see what women would identify as their biggest struggle or roadblock. Wouldn't you know it, over 90 percent of the women (and some men) answered back with some sort of "fear of failure." They didn't want to fail at school, in their marriage, as a parent, in their jobs, as a friend, etc. You name it, they worried they would inevitably fail. Many were too afraid to pursue their God-given dreams for fear of failing at those, too. They couldn't see past the shade of the tree to something they knew God had purposed them to step out and do. There is something worse than failure, and that's the fear of failure, which can kill hopes and paralyze you. I've seen it happen many times. It will do more harm, kill more dreams, and ruin more lives than failure ever will.

Why do we let fear rule us? Could it be our past failures? Are we still listening to old scripts about them? Are we letting them rule us from years past?

Laura knew God called her to start a business, and her passion for women telling their stories ran deep. I could hear it in her voice as we talked. The Lord had given her a dream, and it spilled out over everything she did and said. She desired to help women own their stories and meet Jesus in powerful new ways. She could change the world. I dreamed of coaching clients like this, women ready to run. But Laura had one small spot where she kept getting stuck. This point seemed so important to her, but in the big scheme of things, it didn't matter. The details held her down and hindered her ability to turn her dreams into action. The calling and direction were clear, but Laura lacked a name for her ministry. Should she use her own name? Would that make the ministry too self-focused? Should it be something beautiful, empowering, or light and fun? Too many options caused her to freeze, as if the name determined her success. That's where I jumped in and helped her uncover that she actually already knew the answer. Deep down in her gut, it was clear. And, phew, the name she chose sounded beautiful. Laura hoped for women to find revival in their lives and hearts, and it made sense for her ministry name to share the same wording. How empowering for women to be revived into a new life and direction. We settled on "Her Revival," and the fire in her voice roared with the freedom of this weight lifted. I couldn't wait to see how God used her. When we hung up from our session, she had a clear plan and direction to take her ministry by force.

Months later, I found out that Laura had yet to officially settle on a name, and still she sat undecidedly stuck. What seemed a simple and clear step, an easy win, sent her into a tailspin. My heart broke for her. Laura couldn't move past the idea phase for fear of a wrong business name, and because of that, her ministry never started. What she couldn't see was that the name didn't matter. But what she dreamed of setting out to do and how she planned to help change the lives of women *did* matter. What held her back? Why couldn't she move forward?

She put too much weight on a name. It had to be perfect, or else. Which is another way of saying that she feared failing. Often, we claim failure before we have even taken the fall. Because we have failed before, we believe we are capable of nothing more than failing. Because our worth has been measured by a pile of shortcomings and mess-ups, we don't think we're good enough for the thing we are called to. We can't be wrong because we believe we are "bad" if we mess up. Like Ricky Bobby in *Talladega Nights* says, "If you ain't first, you're last."[1] And if we fail, we're last.

Laura, wrapped with the notion of perfection, could not take a step. Because she never took a step, her dreams (you know, the ones God gave her) never became a reality. Years wasted, dreams forgotten, a life left unchanged.

Yes, there is pain in failure. It can cut deep, leaving scars and reminders like a breakdancing move gone wrong. It can haunt us with our past decisions or current circumstances—a part of our stories that won't let go and can't be forgotten. Rather than risk feeling this again, we run and hide, never moving forward while our negative script screams in our head: *Do you see how you've messed up? Nothing good could ever come of you again. You're a failure.*

We all mess up. We all make mistakes—that's the human condition. But God promised the prophet something deeply encouraging. Just as Isaiah wanted to throw in the towel as his nation was heading toward imminent exile, God said this: "Don't be afraid, for I am with you. Don't be discouraged, for I am your God. I will strengthen you and help you. I will hold you up with my victorious right hand" (Isa. 41:10 NLT). This is true for you as well. God is with you. He will strengthen you—even when you fail.

Note

[1] *Talladega Nights: The Ballad of Ricky Bobby*, directed by Adam McKay (2006; Culver City, CA: Sony Pictures Releasing).

CHAPTER 2

New Script:

I AM NOT A FAILURE

Have you ever blown up a balloon and watched it take form? There's an anxious anticipation that comes over you as the end nears. It's a delicate balance of not wanting to underfill your balloon and getting as much air in as possible. But then, which often happens to me at the last second, pop! There goes the balloon.

So, I called Bob Goff.

You know, the big-time, full-of-life bestselling author, speaker, and color guy?! The self-proclaimed "Chief Balloon Inflator"? Yeah, that one. I called him. On just another Friday, when the rest of the world concerned itself with lunch plans, finishing out meetings, and preparing for the weekend, I clutched his book, *Dream Big*, trying to psych myself into dialing his number. My fingers were numb, my pulse raced, and anxiety churned my stomach until I came close to spewing the contents of my lunch on our cream-colored carpet. As you may know, Bob Goff publicly publishes his phone number in his books, by the way. He encourages people to call. He can't often answer, but I figured, why not try?

Knowing what to say to Bob wouldn't be a problem for me. Sam and I spent the twenty minutes prior to this moment writing down bullet points, rehearsing my "script," and deciding what my plan of action would be if the call went to voicemail. My hands trembled. What if he didn't answer? Or even worse, what if he did? "Bob says, 'When you call me, you have my undivided attention, but you only have it for so long,'" I told Sam. "How do you even stick out to a man who receives over one hundred calls a day?" Also, what human purposefully and excitedly attempts to answer his phone that many times a day? Why call someone when you can text them? That's my motto in life. But Bob, he's different.

So, we thought of ideas of how to stand out. "When he answers, yell 'peacock, peacock, peacock,'" Sam suggested. "Then say, 'Now that I have your attention, this is what I have to say.'" In that moment, I realized that Sam may be a touch crazy and may also have a little hidden genius. I'm not sure Bob has ever had a phone call rival that of a woman screaming bird names at him.

Just hit the button, Brittany, I told myself.

I froze, afraid to move. I couldn't dial the number, because everyone knew him and he had the potential to change my world. But what if he didn't deem my dreams and ambitions worthy enough to help? I would look foolish and branded with a giant letter "F" for failure. *Even Bob Goff, the happiest man in the world, rejected her.* But what if the key to my success belonged to him? I had to know. Before I knew it, my shaky fingers dialed the number.

The phone rang, and he picked up. He actually answered the phone. Was this real life? Our conversation was a complete blur. I'm not sure of everything I told Bob. Maybe I offered to be his best friend, cook him dinner, or wash his car. I'm uncertain of these things. But I do remember the fact that I rambled on the whole time. Poor Bob, a man of many words, and I wouldn't let him use any of them. After saying everything I could think of all over the phone and into his ear, I paused nervously.

After what felt like an eternity, he asked me to email him with more information. *Wait, did he really just say that?* Surely, he spoke politely, trying to get off the phone without hurting my feelings. That's what I kept telling myself, but secretly, I felt hopeful. Can you imagine getting to work with Bob Goff and having him sign off on your dream? *Bob and Brittany: a cheerful, bright force to be reckoned with.* That night, I sent an email full of my passions, thoughts, and what I'd love his help with. There was nothing left for me to type when I finally hit send, and, just for good measure, I included a brief bio with a fun headshot of myself. You know, to highlight the pink hair. That should scream, *Hey, I'm a fun gal, work with me!* Then I waited for a few days.

My wrist dinged with a notification that I had received an email. Could it be? Yes, a reply from Bob. Can you believe he actually emailed me? *We're practically best friends now,* I thought.

Or not.

Hi Brittany,

Great to hear from you. You've got some really beautiful ambitions and I can tell you've got a lot of energy around them too! I hope you'll keep throwing everything you've got at them!

I've got a pretty full plate as it sounds like you do too, so I'm not going to be able to take anything new on, but I can affirm for you what you already know—there are tons of people hoping you'll bring your message to them!

Bob Goff
Chief Balloon Inflator

Pop. There went my balloon.

I sent a screenshot of my rejection to a friend with the comment, "Well, there's that," as tears filled my eyes. The defeat suffocated, my head swirled with doubt, and I collapsed feeling certain of one thing: I felt ridiculous to believe any of this a possibility. *Why do I keep trying to chase this dream?* While many would see Bob's kind and affirming response as sweet support, at the time, I saw his words as a door slamming shut on my hope and future. I had given him the power to make my dreams a reality, which led me to feel like a joke.

My friend's reply, though, was something I'll never forget.

He might be "chief balloon inflator" (or deflator in this case) but the bottom line is Bob Goff didn't call you to this, God did. You don't need Bob's support or backing, and I'm pretty sure God wants you to be clear on that. Would it be nice? Yeah. Does God need his help? No. So feel bummed for a day. It's okay to be disappointed. Then get right back to looking at the faces of who needs to hear what God has told you to say. And say it.

She spoke truth. Would it have been nice, a story for the ages? Yes. But I'm starting to think God has a bigger plan, one that only he could get the credit for. That's what I'm choosing to believe. Here it is, friends: your God-given dreams don't need approval or validation from anyone, no matter how famous. God doesn't need any help from them either. He's got this. Bob's great, and one day I'm sure we'll be good friends—wouldn't that be amazing? What has this call taught me? Not to let someone else's script dictate your direction. Clear the noise, pop all the distractions, and look for the One whose opinions and thoughts matter.

The sinking feeling of failure is real. I can attest to moments when that script was the only one I could hear, and the cry blared so loud, I doubted my worth and everything I ever believed. Do you also know that feeling? I know I'm not alone in this. Talking with women all the time, I hear them plagued with past failures, big and small. Those shortcomings, mistakes, or failures have broken them. They have made them fragile shells of the women God created them to be. Yes, I know that feeling. I've listened to that script, and I've been crushed by it before. Just like you.

So here I sit, writing this book to you, the book Bob passed on, but the one we all need. I could have let his dismissal stop me. I could have let his "no" script ring louder in my ears than the urgency and passion God has given me. But I've done that before. What I found, hidden in the rejection and overshadowed by the failure, was the fact that I was the one who was suffering.

I wanted to try something different this time. What did I have to lose? This time, the "no" would allow me to be braver, fear less about what others' reactions or my setbacks might be, and focus on the calling in front of me. That calling is you, and I want you to be brave with me.

Maybe you don't believe there can be a future or hope outside of your current reality. Maybe you're thinking, *That's great, Brittany, but I don't think it will work for me. My failure wasn't a silly phone call, a tanked business, or even the fear of something scary. No, I really messed up my life.*

Okay, but what if I told you that I know a guy—you know, in my best mobster shrug, lips curled, raspy whisper kind of way. Because I do. I know a guy named David who messed up big-time. Maybe you've read about him in the Bible.

King David was a man respected and loved by many. He had almost everything he could ever want. But here's the problem: he wanted a married woman. Almost as if it were a plot twist in a romance movie, the woman ended up pregnant. David messed up, and, in a panic, he scrambled to cover up what he had done. "David wrote a letter to Joab and gave it to Uriah to deliver. The letter instructed Joab, 'Station Uriah on the front lines where the battle is the fiercest. Then pull back so that he will be killed'" (2 Sam. 11:14–15 NLT).

I once walked into my kitchen to see my two-year-old and my entire kitchen floor covered in powdered sugar—like Santa had dropped the north pole off right in my house. As I looked at my little man, eyelids heavy from the weight of the white powder, chest covered, wearing only a diaper, clearly trying to mask the mess behind him, I asked Ethan what happened, to which he replied, "Nothing." That "nothing" looked like a whole lot of something that I was going to have to clean up.

That, too, was King David, but on a much larger scale. He was stuck in his mistake, covered in powder, and trying to hide it. But instead of owning up, he had the woman's husband killed. Just like my toddler, he thought nobody would ever know. But God knew, and he sent a messenger to tell David. Once David realized the jig was up and the weight of what he had done hit him, he was crushed. This man, once known for slaying giants and killing vicious animals, crumbled at his great failure. "Then David confessed to Nathan, 'I have sinned against the LORD.'

Nathan replied, 'Yes, but the LORD has forgiven you, and you won't die for this sin'" (2 Sam. 12:13 NLT).

Have you found yourself crushed by the weight of your failures, especially the ones that seem so earthshaking and huge? Me too. But here's what I need you to see. David didn't just hang up his robe, call it a day, and lie around waiting to die. No, he owned his failures, cried out to God, and begged him to make things right in his heart again, to clean up the powdered sugar mess like I had to for Ethan. "God, make a fresh start in me . . . Don't throw me out with the trash, or fail to breathe holiness in me. Bring me back from gray exile, put a fresh wind in my sails!" (Ps. 51:10–12 *The Message*).

David's sin and cover-up didn't define his entire life. His actions did have severe consequences (see 2 Samuel 12:10–12 for the graphic repercussions), but, as we see in Scripture, we know David for so much more. In fact, he's known for being a man after God's own heart. That's what we remember him for. And can I tell you something? You have the chance to start afresh too, my friend. The road won't be easy, there may be consequences, and Satan will try to remind you of your failures at every step forward. But you can get back up, and your past doesn't have to define you. If we follow Jesus, we know that sin and our old lives no longer control us; we are new people. Like 2 Corinthians 5:17 says, "This means that anyone who belongs to Christ has become a new person. The old life is gone; a new life has begun!" (NLT). It's not just the old life that's gone; so is the weight of our negative scripts.

We have a goldendoodle named Walt, and he is the cutest, most precious dog in the world. Yes, I know you thought that title belonged to your pup. Sorry to disappoint you, but it does not. Walt is just the best. He and I love to go on runs together. He looks forward to them every day. I cannot come out of my bedroom dressed in workout clothes without him attacking me, eager to head out for a run. He knocks me over as I stretch, weaving in and out around my body as it bends like a pretzel. It's quite comical. But once we finally head out the door on our run, he is straight business. Many times, that guy pulls me along for *his* run. I've been known to clock a 4:40 mile with Walt at the helm.

Without fail, though, every time we go on our runs, Walt can be counted on to poop. He is not sorry to stop, drop, and relieve himself no matter where we are or who is around. This is just a fact of life for him. Is it annoying to stop midstride to allow him to handle his business? Yes. Does it stink? Yes. Do I wish I didn't have to deal with the aftermath? Yes. But just because the action Walt partakes in every run is "crap," I'm not going to label him a "crapper." *Hey friends, have you met my little crapper?* No, he is so much more than that. His worth isn't defined by that one act. Instead, when I think of Walt, I think of my best friend, my cuddle partner, and a straight-up joy to be around.

The same is true with failure. Failing is an action and a stinky one at that. But somehow, somewhere, we have adopted the term *failure* to go along with it. *Failure* is a label of shame, one we use to devalue our lives, abilities, and worth. *Hi, my name is Brittany, and I'm a failure.* That one word packs together all of our shortcomings, mess-ups, inadequacies, and crap. It's a weight we seem to own, cling to, and carry.

But what if we don't have to?

Sister, if I were face-to-face with you right now, I'd grab your shoulders, lock eyes with you, and preach truth to your heart. I'm sorry that you have listened to a failure script for so long. I'm sorry that you feel your worth is defined by your abilities to succeed or please others. I'm sorry that you find yourself hidden in rejection and overshadowed by failure.

Here's what I need you to know. You are not a failure, and you are worth far more than you give yourself credit for. I know, because I've seen it played out in my life and the lives of many women I've had the pleasure of meeting, women like my friend Robin.

I first learned about Robin when I was hidden in the back row of an auditorium, legs crossed, coffee in one hand and a pen in the other, poised to take notes. I sat in a room full of women ready to hear from our keynote speaker and conference host, Jess. I had known Jess for years, when we were mommy bloggers back in the day, popping out kids like some people pop Tic Tacs.

As the retreat kicked off, Jess pulled out a letter. It was written on white copy paper and folded into thirds—nothing special or extravagant—but the contents of that handwritten note wrecked me. It was a letter from Robin.

Through some less-than-great life choices, Robin found herself in prison. But somewhere during her sentence, Jesus got hold of her heart, and she became a different woman. She was ready to change her life and make a difference in the lives of many after she left the walls of her cell. Through her letter, she explained that she had been able to read one of Jess's books and that she related to the part about rejection. As her release date neared, Robin spent her time reaching out to organizations and churches in hopes of making connections and wanting to find help to stay on her new path. But all she had been met with was silence. This girl, desperate to start afresh, reached out to anyone who could help.

She went on to share that her prison started a seminary for the inmates. But Robin didn't qualify for the program because she would be released soon. Her cellmate, a student of the seminary, let her borrow the books to read along. The words she read challenged her, changed her, and gave her hope for the future. They reminded her that even though she had messed up greatly, she *still* had a purpose, in this season, for this time. Her life would not be over.

I cried. This woman was my hero. She faced all of the reasons to feel like a failure, and yet she still held a glimmer of hope and a passion for her future. She flipped her script. The old script declared she wouldn't amount to anything, but her new script reminded her of her future in Christ. I have never wanted to hug, hold, or coach someone so badly in my life. I grabbed a notecard and feverishly wrote down everything bubbling up in my heart. The odds of ever meeting Robin appeared slim, but that didn't stop me. I wanted to send a little bit of hope back to her. Although she felt alone, I wanted her to carry these words with her forever, reminding her of truth. This girl had a new balloon and chance at life, and I pictured myself cheering for her as she attempted to breathe new air into it. With all my might, I yelled through the pen and paper:

Hey friend,

I am so proud of you! There has been a seed planted, a desire in your heart, and a spark lit. Don't let anything stop you. Lies will try to present themselves as truth, your past will try to derail you, and rejection may come. But, there is no failure and no struggle that God will not use for

your good and His glory. He is mighty in you and
He gets the final say. I'm cheering for you!

Your friend,
Brittany

Robin will be a world changer; I can feel it in my jellies. That's
a term my daughter says when she believes something is going
to be great. It's like her gut feeling. I love the term so much,
because sometimes you need more than your gut—you need
to believe it all the way in your jellies.

I know that sometimes our minds are the most brutal place
to be. There we concoct scripts like, *You'll always mess up.*
You'll never succeed. You deserve this setback. If we stay with
these negative scripts, we are apt to live them. The author of
Proverbs reminds us how important our hearts are: "Guard
your heart above all else, for it determines the course of your
life" (Prov. 4:23 NLT).

The script rolling around in our heads can tear us down
and tell us who we are and what we aren't. It can make us feel
defeated, overwhelmed, insecure, and worthless. Before we
know it, the loop playing over and over sends us into a toxic
spiral. Consider the following negative scripts. Perhaps you
relate? And then choose the positive scripts based on the Bible
that will help you retrain your mind toward the freedom and
joy Jesus has for you.

- **Old script:** *I will never amount to anything.* **New
  script:** *Because of what Jesus did for me, I have a
  brand-new life* (2 Cor. 5:17).
- **Old script:** *I deserve this struggle.* **New script:** *God
  promises to work all things out for my good and his
  glory* (Rom. 8:28).

- **Old script:** *All I do is mess up.* **New script:** *God's grace is all I need because God's power works best in my weaknesses* (2 Cor. 12:9).
- **Old script:** *I am too afraid.* **New script:** *God has not given me a spirit of fear, but one of power, love, and sound mind* (2 Tim. 1:7).

You are not merely the sum of your thoughts. You *can* overcome the familiar scripts you have wrongly believed as truth. John promises us, "You, dear children, are from God and have overcome them, because the one who is in you is greater than the one who is in the world" (1 John 4:4 NIV). With the strength of the Holy Spirit who resides in you, you can rewrite the script you listen to and can release the ideals of perfection. You are going to mess up, make mistakes, and get things wrong. But this does not make you a failure. This makes you a human. You are worth far too much to believe anything less.

You have a chance; you have a future. Dispel the negative scripts trying to take root in your heart. Believe that God will use all of this for your good and his glory. And keep moving forward. God is not done, and Paul reminds us of this in Philippians 1:6: "And I am certain that God, who began the good work within you, will continue his work until it is finally finished on the day when Christ Jesus returns" (NLT). Below are some practical ways to transform your scripts.

Find the Triggers

Notice when your thoughts start bringing you down. What's going on when this happens? Who's around you? Pinpoint the harmful words and write out your negative script. This will help you determine the root cause lurking beneath—something every bad thought has. Most of the time, your negative script is buried deep in a lie you are believing. But you can't work to change the script unless you first call out the root lie and dialogue beneath it all.

Finish the Statement

Conclude your negative script with the words "in Jesus's name." If the statement you're believing doesn't sound right when it's followed by "in Jesus's name," then it probably isn't true. (For example: *Man, I am so dumb . . . in Jesus's name.*) It is amazing how quickly you can pick out lies by using this tool. The words spoken about you partnered with the name of Jesus should never make you feel broken and filled with shame. They should make you feel seen and loved.

Seek Truth

Find truth to replace the lie. My favorite thing to do is create a list of scriptures that I can go to when my mind starts to spiral. Grab a small index-size spiral notebook, and write down the negative script you struggle with. As you pray and find scriptures that combat your old script, write them down. A small notebook is perfect to throw in your purse/backpack, keep in your car, or even have on your desk at work. It's the perfect reminder and way to tangibly flip your script. Nothing fights fear, doubt, worthlessness, or overwhelm like the Word of God! Read your scripture list out loud to yourself because there's power in those words. I've been known to paste verses on my mirror, in my car, and even on the wall in front of my toilet. It's a good way to keep busy. Fun fact: I do this for my kids as well. On big state-testing days for them, I write affirmations, verses, etc. on their arms with a Sharpie. It's reassurance for them when they need it most.

Speak Up

Talk to safe people. This may include a counselor, pastor, family member, or friend. Find someone you trust who can call out these negative scripts and help you find truth. No good comes from battling lies in silence. If you don't have a safe person, call me. My phone number is listed in the back of this book, just for you. I will be that person for you. I'm not kidding; I took a note from Bob Goff and posted my number on social media. You are not alone, you will never be alone, and if you can't see past the fear, call me. Or shoot, if you want to discuss your love of coffee and Mexican food, you can call me about that too. Because I always want to talk.

Friends, our minds are battlefields. Some days will feel like winning, and others will look a lot like surviving. But one thing is certain: if you are a follower of Christ, the battle is already won. Suit up and claim that victory, because, sister, according to the Word of God, you are *not* a failure.

CHAPTER 3

Old Script:
I AM UNWORTHY

The first time I met Sarah, I was in awe. She was so beautiful and well-dressed, and she projected confidence in everything she said and did. This girl was the definition of classy. Even as adults, I knew that she and I ran in different crowds. I was the scrappy, crazy girl who made people laugh, so it came as a complete surprise when, a year later, we ended up becoming best friends. How in the world?! Sarah was not only the classiest lady I had ever met on the outside, but her heart and compassion rivaled none. She wanted to love Jesus with her whole heart and live her life in such a way that others couldn't deny his presence.

A few years into our friendship, we found ourselves heading home from a women's retreat. I was driving because there weren't any time constraints on us arriving back home. Sarah had a lead foot, and she likened my driving to a *maw-maw*, a term of endearment she loved to call me. "Oh, it's maw-maw behind the wheel," or "I'll drive because we don't have time for maw-maw to." She loved me, and I didn't mind in the slightest being referred to as a slow-driving grandma.

There is something you should know about me: I don't speed. I'd like to say it's a personal conviction to do the right thing, but it's nothing honorable like that. Actually, I'm afraid of being pulled over by a cop. They make me so nervous, like clammy palms, pits sweating, shaky voice, and tears in my eyes kind of anxiety. Listen, you never know if their speedometers are off when they clock you, and I cannot get a ticket. The mere act of them flipping their lights on may just cause me to keel over right then and there. In light of all of this, I'd rather be extra cautious and drive a few miles *under* the limit. Better safe than sorry, right? It's okay, maw-maw will get us where we need to go.

As we cruised down the highway—at a safe speed, of course—we discussed all of the things we learned over the previous days. I loved our conversations together. It was nice to be real with someone and know she was being real as well. Sarah began to share about times in her past when she felt shame, pain, and hurt, including moments of correction from her father that caused her to cower in his presence, all for typical childish things like breaking a vase, fighting with her sister, or kissing a boy. This strong woman I knew and loved crumbled as she described times of not measuring up, that she could never be the girl her parents—especially her father—wanted. There was nothing remarkable about her, she informed me, questioning how she even caught the attention of her husband. Tears filled Sarah's eyes as she reached for a tissue and began to tell me the story of her affair. The words flying out of her mouth degraded herself and the choices of her past. She talked of the beauty and restoration that had since come from that mistake all of those years ago, but the scale appeared unbalanced to her. She didn't deserve her husband, and she didn't know if she deserved any of the good people in her life. Even more, she couldn't understand how God would choose to love her.

But I couldn't shake the sinking feeling as she shared that I, too, had felt that before. Those memories cut her deep; I could hear it in her voice. That's when I looked over at her and said, "Sarah, I think the root of all of these feelings boil down to your worth. You feel unworthy." Then I began to explain what I heard her share with me. Each memory was a piece of evidence, evidence of a case she was ultimately losing. As much as she tried to bury these memories, they were beginning to consume her. She was dying as she believed those lies and accepted them as truth.

The car fell silent. *Oh gosh.* I questioned whether I had said too much, made her mad, or, maybe, suddenly one of us became deaf. The last option was less likely, but you never know, crazier things have happened. I looked over at Sarah, and I knew she heard me; I could see the tears forming in her eyes. Something clicked inside of her. To the core, she knew this was how she felt. But what was worse than realizing these things was not knowing how to fix them. I could see it on her face. How was she supposed to fix a problem that had woven itself so intricately through her life?

She needed to believe that she was worthy, worthy enough for God to love. She knew he loved her, but she couldn't fully accept the idea that he saw value in who she was. Somewhere along the line, the truth of who God created her to be and what he thought of her became twisted. Shame entered the picture, and she felt that her worth was diminished. Yes, she made mistakes. No, she wasn't perfect. No, she couldn't measure up to a God who was. But God knew she couldn't, and, in his kindness, he called her worthy. She was worth bridging the gap and making a way for her to be his forever. But where was she supposed to go from here? I didn't know what else to say, so I simply said, "Oh Sarah, we are going to figure this out."

Maybe you have felt like this, too? Have you felt that sinking feeling in the pit of your stomach when you felt like you just didn't measure up? Have there been moments when you've never been surer of your completely worthless existence? These could be fleeting thoughts or ones that plague your mind daily. Either way, you're not alone.

I come across women all the time who question their value and worth. Whether I'm on a stage teaching hundreds of women about their purpose or coaching them one-on-one, this seems to be a topic we can't avoid. It's the ultimate negative script. Because if you believe you have no value and no worth and that you'll never measure up, the enemy doesn't have to distract you any other way. Here's the problem—we have forgotten who we are. We're like the price-check station at Target, scanning ourselves over and over again hoping the results will make us whole. But for some reason or another, the price we see never satisfies us. Why is that? Listen, those stations are super handy and I love a good sale (can I get an amen?). In fact, I pride myself on scoring the best deals for my holiday shopping. But, despite popular belief, Target doesn't have all the answers. Target is not where you shop to understand and know your worth. No, that answer can't be found in the world; it's discovered in God's Word. Paul wrote to the Romans, telling them about how to truly learn to flip their negative script: "Don't copy the behavior and customs of this world, but let God transform you into a new person by changing the way you think. Then you will learn to know God's will for you, which is good and pleasing and perfect" (Rom. 12:2 NLT).

In high school, I had the biggest crush on teen heartthrob Heath Ledger. He was the cutest. He had dark, shaggy hair; a perfect Australian accent; and a smile that could melt you like a popsicle in the July Texas heat. I made it my mission to watch all of the movies he starred in. It was like a sport to me. Then I proceeded to dream about the day when we would actually meet and he would inevitably fall in love with me. *Mrs. Brittany Ledger*, I could see it now. Of course, it was a one in a million chance, but I remembered the words of Lloyd from *Dumb and Dumber*: "So you're saying there's a chance!"[1] To me, it was possible. When the movie *A Knight's Tale* opened in theaters, I claimed a front-row seat. It was perfection on a screen, and it solidified my desire to become Heath's bride.

In case you've been deprived of this rom-com genius, let me break it down for you. A peasant boy named William dreams of one day becoming a great knight. He hopes to "change the stars" and create a different future for himself. I can't fault him; I've often wished I could change my stars as well. Thankfully, I'm not stuck in medieval times and desperate for food after the sudden passing of my master. That's when he and his fellow servant buddies come up with a plan. They are going to fake William's royal lineage so he can compete in tournaments to earn money, fame, and a chance to be a real knight. As I'm sure you know, like any good romance movie, there is a beautiful girl that catches the attention of William. Now, he not only wants to win for fame, but also to win her over. It's not long before William's winning streaks at these medieval tournaments catch up to him. All of this attention isn't the best for a man who isn't really a knight, but an imposter. Adhemar, our villain and a man whose ego is so big he'd be the guy caught sweet-talking his own reflection, feels threatened by the accomplishments of William. To make matters worse, he, too, wants the love and affection of William's girl.

William and Adhemar find themselves in an intense jousting match against each other, a real David and Goliath moment—who will come out triumphant? Each man lines up at the start, seated on his horse, lance in hand, with the ultimate goal to defeat the other. As the flag rises and the men begin to charge, the crowd cheers and waits with great anticipation. The same could be said for me, with my bowl of popcorn, Coke in hand, and a stomach full of anxiety. *Would William beat his enemy?!* He had to win; I just knew it. The crowded theater all watched as the men charge on their horses, the lances smash against each other, and wood splinters in all directions. Horror overtook our faces as William flies off his horse and crashes to the ground. Our hopes sank with William's defeat. That's when Adhemar walks over to his opponent, who is still lying on the ground, and says, "You have been weighed, you have been measured, and you have been found wanting."[2] William, wishing for a better future, tries to change his stars, but he comes up short. Adhemar is all too eager to remind him of that fact.

Even to this day, I can remember that quote. Words spoken in a theater by fictional characters, meant for our entertainment, found a place in my heart. When I least expected it, they surfaced and reminded me of what I was and, more importantly, what I wasn't. I was reminded of them when I didn't make the team; when my friends had boyfriends but no guy wanted me, which led me to believe I was ugly; when I didn't meet others' expectations; when pictures on social media reminded me of parties I wasn't invited to and outings I didn't make the cut for; when others appeared incredibly successful and the only thing I successfully did was hear the word "no."

I thought about that movie and those words as I sat down for my first counseling session. On a teal sectional full of fun pillows, I had no idea where to sit. *Do I go to the end? Maybe I should sit in the middle? Do I lean all the way back? Curl up like I'm going to watch a movie? And why are there so many pillows?* The corner in the middle was where I settled, with my elbows resting on my knees as I leaned forward, prepped for what was to come. Like a football player, I was poised for the snap. That was me, unsure of the opponent's plan, but listening for the quarterback's signal.

Jen was my counselor. She was a tall, beautiful blonde who had a flair for the bohemian and a perfectly eclectic taste that seamlessly reflected throughout her office space. Her face knew no other expression than to smile, and her eyes assured me she really saw me and loved who I was, right in that moment. I loved Jen's quiet confidence. Her presence calmed my racing heart. You need people in your life who make you feel seen, and Jen saw me. I mean, technically, I paid her to do that, but who's splitting hairs?

The first time I sat in her office, I blurted out that I wasn't mad to be there. I thought she should know that, even though counseling hadn't been *my* choice. Instead, the decision found me as a mandate for my job at the time after a crazy summer where burnout became my reality. I had nothing against counseling and definitely could use the time with her, but the circumstances around my arrival to that teal couch were less than ideal. Either way, I nervously clutched onto a bright orange fuzzy pillow and cracked a joke. Because that's what we Enneagram sevens do. When things get too heavy, you can trust us to come in clutch with a lighthearted comment to break the tension and make you laugh.

In case you are unfamiliar with the Enneagram, here's a quick explanation:

> **The Enneagram** is a system that shows us the nine ways that the people in the world default to in life. The Enneagram explains the "why" of all that we do, think, and feel. These nine types are based on our core motivations. When we delve into the Enneagram we can better understand ourselves and begin to grow.[3]

Type sevens are known for their fun-loving, adventurous natures. They are the enthusiasts, walking parties in human form. While they can usher in the fun like no one else, they try to avoid pain. Who likes pain, anyway? That's when you'll see a typical seven (hand raised) quickly rush in with a joke or funny story. If you ask me, Enneagram sevens are the real MVPs.

Clearly, Jen had her work cut out for her. I assured her that I was ready for all that therapy had to offer. *Fix this hot-mess girl up.* Clearly people *did* think I was a hot mess, or they wouldn't have asked me to go to therapy, so in my mind, there was no place but up from here. Glass half-full, baby! (I told you I'm a seven.) I meant every word of that *hot mess girl* statement, but I didn't realize the weight it carried. Oh, how that negative script wrote itself all over my life. After a few awkwardly clumsy moments full of my jokey dodging tactics, I settled in and opened up.

My times with Jen were both brutal and lifegiving all at once. She let me walk through rough moments when negative thoughts continued to play a loop in my mind, leaving me stuck. Like fog lifting on an early fall morning, it took a few sessions for clarity to come. I discovered the root issue, which was my own negative script playing in my mind.

Something is wrong with me.

Tears fell down my cheeks and onto my jeans as I admitted my discovery to Jen. Words that I could barely get out of my mouth felt at home in my heart, like an unwanted and unnamed houseguest taking up residence even after the party is over. It was true—I've always felt this way. But why?

I've never been good at fitting in, sometimes not for lack of trying, but it seems, instead, I'm good at being different. Growing up, my grandpa would tease me every time we'd visit him. Like clockwork, at our first meal together (my grandma's ham balls, if we were lucky [heaven on a plate]), he'd see my hand grab the fork and pipe up, "Brittany, I'm right-handed, what are you?" After all the years, I knew our routine.

I'd reply, "I'm left-handed, Grandpa!"

Then he'd snicker, saying, "Brittany, if you're not right-handed, then what are you?"

Confused, I'd look over to my parents, wishing they'd save me from this exchange.

"Grandpa, I'm left-handed." This would go on a few more times until I was certain the world had created a new label for this phenomenon of writing with one's left hand. In a gasp of defeat, I'd give up.

"If you're not right-handed, then you're *wrong*-handed!" And he'd laugh, proud of his dad joke. I, however, being the only lefty in my family, felt like something was wrong with me. Did he know this script was written over my heart? Not even in the slightest, but it's funny how moments like that happen without your permission, without your knowledge. Suddenly, you can't see past them.

In school, teachers would call me out for talking loud in class: "Your voice just carries, Brittany." Boys always put me in the friend zone: "I'm sorry, Brittany; you're like one of the guys to me." Most days, I walked the halls of our campus in a T-shirt, basketball shorts, and flip-flops. Some days, I'd even show up in the scrubs I used years prior as a junior volunteer at our local hospital. Hot stuff, I know. I even boycotted makeup for a bit in high school because I told people I wanted a guy who would be happily surprised when I did wear it, not petrified when I didn't. They needed to know what they were getting themselves into. Feeling too much, too young, too old, too loud, too bossy, etc. felt like home to me. You name it, I was never "just right." And just like the children's story with Goldilocks and the three bears, I found myself as a pink-haired "goldilocks" looking for her "just right" baby bear, to no avail. This didn't stop after high school, but man, how I wish it did. Who knew people still act like high schoolers even as grown adults?! News to me. As rejection came, situations became rough, friendships blew up, and so on. These negative scripts played like a broken record in my head.

It's your fault they don't want to be your friend. You are too loud for people. Why can't you act like so-and-so? You're no stranger to this feeling, are you? And when we hear these scripts long enough, we believe they must be true, and we allow them to take root deep down. Just like Sarah's car ride confession, everything clicked for me in the office with my counselor. Something was wrong with me. That discovery felt like a fatal blow. I had been knocked to the ground and was gasping for air. I had been weighed and measured and was ultimately found wanting. But that's not how the story ends. Like Paul writes in Philippians, "I'm sure about this: the one who started a good work in you will stay with you to complete the job by the day of

Christ Jesus" (Phil. 1:6 CEB). We can trust that God, who finds you worthy of the sacrifice of his own son, will be with you and help you see it for yourself.

Notes

[1] *Dumb and Dumber*, directed by Peter Farrelly (1994; Burbank, CA: New Line Cinema).

[2] *A Knight's Tale*, directed by Brian Helgeland (2001; Culver City, CA: Sony Pictures Releasing).

[3] Enneagram Explained, https://enneagramexplained.com/.

CHAPTER 4

New Script:

I AM WORTHY

"There's something wrong with me."

I blurted it out without a chance to temper or comprehend the words I spoke. Like a hiccup I couldn't contain, it escaped my lips and filled the air around me. It's a phrase that my mind, and more importantly, my heart, couldn't shake. It was tough to hear, but in that instant, nothing sounded more true. In a room full of eclectic colors and floral designs, I, tucked into a couch covered in pillows that acted as my shield, found the words for the first time. My eyes, full of desperation, looked at my counselor like they were calling out to her for rescue. *What do I do with this feeling?* That realization brought waves of validation, almost a settling, into me because "it" had a name, coupled with the rush of suffocation. The dichotomy of those feelings left me perplexed.

The belief that something was wrong with me was like a thread I could see woven through my life. While it seemed remarkable to put a phrase to my struggle, I wondered how this mindset could be overcome? Years of training, self-dialogue, and hurt had created a powerful negative script that I lived by. But I was determined to feel whole. I wouldn't allow Satan to have this stronghold anymore. But now what?

That's when my brilliant counselor spoke up. Her tone instantly put me at ease, even if I didn't quite see truth in her words. She told me to speak the exact opposite over myself. Yes, it felt as foolish as it sounds, like a self-help, new-age guru seeking for someone to love herself and unlock the key to her superpower. We sat together for a while as I tried my hardest to let the words "I am perfect just the way I am" soak in. Nothing changed. The words seemed superficial, trite, and ineffective. Seeing my distress, she had me flip the script. "This time, picture Jesus sitting next to you on the fluffy teal couch, holding your face, and saying the same thing over you." With my eyes closed, I pictured Jesus grabbing my cheeks and pulling them close like I often did to my little ones when I wanted to whisper something sweet or kiss their cheeks. He whispered the words over me like imparting a secret—my secret, a truth I craved—to a treasured friend. Without a second thought, I began to cry. While I struggled to speak it over myself, something switched when I pictured Jesus saying it to me. I couldn't deny it. He breathed new life into me while he broke down all the hurtful things that had taken root deep down. It was just a quiet and simple moment, but so powerful.

Through the process of flipping the script in my own life, I've resigned myself to certain facts. My personality is a lot to handle; it's fun, but it's also strong. I'm a natural leader, and nothing energizes me more than taking the stage. That's how

God created me, and I'm good at it. For so long, I felt stuck in the tension of who I was and what others expected and accepted of me. But you see, I can't anymore. The Lord has brought on such freedom in my life, and I couldn't stop if I tried. This freedom has ignited courage in my heart to fight for freedom. I don't have the luxury to live afraid and stay stuck in negative scripts, especially if it keeps me (and you) from freedom. That's not God's desire, either.

Maybe your script sounds similar to mine? This is what I want to encourage you to do. Find a quiet place, and stop. Close your eyes, take a deep breath, and slowly let the air fill your lungs while you lift your chest, shoulders, and head like they are attached to an invisible marionette string. Your countenance changes with the exhale. Now, listen for the Lord with all your might. He's there. Let him grab you by the cheeks, pull you in close, and whisper the truth of your worth. Let it wash over you and tear down all the negative scripts you're holding onto. Then believe him. You are his gift and treasured one.

Trips to the store were a favorite activity of mine as a kid—not because I loved shopping, but because I knew that I possessed the skills to talk my parents into a trip down the toy aisle during our outing. It's a gift I hold dear, and if you pay me enough, I may be able to teach you my ways. One day, during an outing to the store, I again sweet-talked my way down to the toy section. As we turned the corner from the beauty supply section, passing the bike racks, building blocks, and bouncy balls, we entered the aisle of stuffed animals. Heaven on Earth, I tell you! So much fluff, color, and sweetness packed into one tiny

section. My eyes skimmed over the lions and tigers, and a bear
. . . oh my. There she was—*my* bear. The bear had white silky
fur and wore a plum velour pantsuit complete with a matching
beret. Perfection in a bear, that's what she was. Grinning from
ear to ear, I quickly grabbed her off the shelf as I bestowed the
only name fitting a classy girl such as her: Samantha. I drank
in her every detail and traced them out with my tiny fingers,
and I promised Samantha that she and I would be inseparable.
Until my mother informed me it was time to go and I needed
to put up my bear. *My bear? Do you mean the stuffed animal of
my dreams, my new best friend, my girl Samantha?!*

In all of our trips to the store, I neglected to remember
that our walks down the toy section involved more moments
of looking and not necessarily buying. This was the flaw in my
plan. I could convince the woman, my mom, to get there, but I
never honed the craft of closing the sale. I usually walked away
empty-handed. How could I not bring Samantha home with
me? Did my mother not see the instant bond we shared? She
crushed my dreams of happiness. I did the only thing my little
second-grade brain knew to do: squeeze Samantha tight and
hide her. I dug deep into the shelf and buried her behind the
other less-appealing animals—the laughable giraffe with the
crazy long neck, the lion wearing glasses, and the puppy in a
polka-dot dress—as if my life depended on it. Surely, nobody
would dig through all these to find my girl. My Samantha would
stay there safely until she could come home with me.

As the holiday season approached, I never forgot about my
lost friend trapped in the store. Did she miss me? Was she okay?
The days passed, and the Christmas tree in our living room
began to be surrounded with beautifully wrapped presents. I
inspected each gift and questioned its size, weight, and potential to house my best friend. Surely, she'd be under there in one

of the packages. When Christmas morning came around, I ran into the living room, tore through my stocking from Santa, and watched my parents pass out everyone's gifts. The stack right in front of me held my Christmas fate. I anxiously bounced up and down in my place, locking eyes on the one box that might have Samantha in it, clenching my fists and teeth as my body tensed with anticipation. Finally, my turn arrived, and I could open my gifts. I couldn't take it any longer. I snatched the box and ripped it to shreds. Paper flew, cardboard split, and there were uncontrollable squeals of a girl who had just opened the present of her dreams. Samantha! I embraced her in tears. She made it home. Her beauty far surpassed anything I remembered at the store. She was everything I ever wanted in one stuffed animal.

Now, almost thirty years later, this story sits fresh in my mind. Never had I wanted a gift so much in my life, and her anticipated arrival on Christmas morning filled me with joy. I wish I could inform you that I still have Samantha to this day. Unfortunately, I don't remember when, but at some point, we gave Samantha away. When I say *give away*, I'm fairly certain we gave her away to the trash can during a spring-cleaning fury a few years later. That's a tragedy.

Gifts are my love language. I love to give them, and I especially love receiving them. Truthfully, who doesn't love a good gift? For me, the best part of the actual gift is the moment before the recipient begins to open the package. The anticipation makes me want to bubble over with excitement, especially when I know I've picked out the perfect gift. But my excitement doesn't even compare to God's excitement on the day of your birth.

Think of it like this: at the beginning of time, God planned out the world. That included you, your life, and your future. Every single moment and detail was accounted for. He smiled at the thought of your laugh, his heart melted at how you would change the world, and he loved every bit of who he created you to be. Then, after he planned the world, he sat back, grabbed a bowl of popcorn, and watched it unfold, waiting for the pinnacle moment of your arrival into the world. I can't be certain God sat and ate popcorn, but shoot, he's God! He can do whatever he wants. I like to think of him like this—eager and ready to see the gift of you. He is the same God who created the mountains, flung the stars in the galaxy, split the Grand Canyon, and hand-picked all of the colors in Hawaii's lush rainforest, and he thought: *Hmm, this world isn't complete without . . . you.*

Then, when the day arrived for you to make your appearance in this world, he couldn't contain himself. He paced around in the delivery room, watched things happen, and checked on updates, eager to meet his girl. In true cinema fashion, the moment you were born, time slowed down, almost to a standstill. People were whirling around and machines were beeping, but none of that mattered. Because here's what I know: your first breath took God's breath away. There you were, a miracle—his daughter, his beautiful baby girl. He had waited so long to see you, and now you were here. Tears filled his eyes as he looked upon your precious face. His love for you is instant and permanent. His love is not based on your accomplishments, if you stumble, or anything of the sort. You are the reason why he sent his Son to die on the cross. He sent his Son not out of guilt or shame, but because his love compelled him. He didn't want to imagine life apart from you, his daughter, his beautiful baby girl. He had waited so long to see you. You are his special one, his favorite, a gift like no other.

My youngest crawled onto the bed and into my lap. With her head to my heart and her body tucked into mine, we sat in silence. Thoughts flooded my mind, but I had no clue how to put them into words and speak. While her father and I were out on a date a few hours earlier, she stayed home with her older siblings. This is something we did often because, thankfully, our kids are older and they can be trusted to hold down the fort for a short period. Or so we thought. That time, while we were out enjoying our dinner, she had become the object of ridicule and pestering, so much so that she found herself hidden under the dining table, chairs pulled in tight, like her fort of safety. There she sat, broken and pleading for us to come home to rescue her.

Before we jump in further, I need you to know that I have great kids. Really and truly, they are the best. But as with all children, they are still working out the kinks of understanding when to stop, especially with the teasing. What they didn't know or take into account was Pippa's emotional barometer from the day. Tiredness from a previous late night, struggles with clothing (that's enough to put anyone in a bad mood, right?), and general insecurities boiled to the surface. When the siblings began to tease without end, she exploded and took solace by hiding under a table.

There we were, curled up together, she and I with her daddy by her side. I took a deep breath, composed my thoughts, and tackled her broken spirit one word at a time. "Pippa, what do you think about your body?" That was a question I dreaded to hear answered because an eight-year-old shouldn't hate her body. Body image shouldn't be a struggle for anyone at any age, but especially not for an eight-year-old little girl.

"I like it." The hesitation in her voice spoke louder than her words.

"Well, I think you have one pretty amazing body, did you know that? You are super strong and make up the best dance moves. Your squishy cheeks and button nose bring a smile to my face. Your eyes of different colors show how unique you are. Your thick hair is stunning, especially with those gray patches. You are remarkable. But Pippa, my favorite part about you is your heart. You have a way of making people laugh, feel loved, and feel like they belong. That is something special." While her daddy and I thought the world of her, we wanted her to understand something important. We don't decide her worth or value. We don't have a say in whether she possesses beauty or talents. Only one gets to make that call, and that's God. Thankfully, her daddy and I agree with everything God has to say.

Grabbing my phone off the bed, I looked up a verse to share. My fingers intuitively typed out the reference and immediately scrolled to it. This verse found its place on my lips often as I quoted it for my own heart. But while I could rattle it off without hesitation, I wanted her to read it for herself. "For we are God's masterpiece. He has created us anew in Christ Jesus, so we can do the good things he planned for us long ago" (Eph. 2:10 NLT). It's right there in plain text: *we are God's masterpiece.* A masterpiece is a priceless work of art. She is a priceless work of art.

As we continued to talk, I stroked her hair and told her that if people teased her or if she heard lies from the enemy, she needed to answer back. The only way to stop the negative dialogue is to find the truth and flip the script. In this case, the lie questioned her worth and value. "Anytime you hear statements that make you question your worth, whether from people or just in your mind, say this: 'That's a lie. I am God's masterpiece.'" Her precious cheeks curled up as a smile formed for the first time in hours. I couldn't stop the battle of her mind or even the words others might say about her, but I could point her to the One who could and then equip her with tools to fight.

Are you struggling, too? For countless women I've talked with, the answer is a resounding yes. Like Pippa, I wish we could sit together, face-to-face, and I could tell you what God thinks of you. More importantly, I'd show you in his Word. You are God's masterpiece. Any statement that leads you to believe otherwise is a lie. Sometimes, when the enemy tries to speak lies over your life, it's easy to get flustered and feel like you need fancy words or actions to fight. It doesn't have to be complicated; it can be as simple as this script: *That's a lie. I am God's masterpiece.* Say it now, say it when you doubt, say it until you believe it. This is truth, and it is truth backed up by God's word.

The idea of a masterpiece is interesting to me. Looking through art history, many of the big names we know all boast works that are deemed masterpieces. Leonardo da Vinci painted *Mona Lisa*, Johannes Vermeer painted *Girl with a Pearl Earring*, Vincent van Gogh painted *The Starry Night*, and the list goes on. These are all incredible works of art we marvel at and study. When I took art history in high school, one painting struck a chord with me. This piece didn't rest on a canvas—it filled the ceiling of the Sistine Chapel in the Vatican. Each year, around six million people tour the chapel and gaze upon this masterpiece. The artist commissioned for the job, Michelangelo, took four years to complete the painting. He spent more than thirty-five thousand hours working to bring his vision to life, so much so that his eyesight became permanently damaged. Can you imagine? Such work, detail, and precision went into that ceiling. Michelangelo gave his all, and hundreds of years later, we can still enjoy it.

Why is it easy for us to look at these pieces of work, made by man, and agree they are breathtaking, but when it comes to who we are, how we look, and how we estimate our worth, we feel more like a bargain store, mass-produced, tacky print? Forget the idea of a masterpiece; most of us don't feel worthy enough for the dollar bin at Target. The same pieces of art that many pay to see were created by brilliant artists who themselves were crafted by the ultimate artist: God. He is the reason any of this beauty exists. The thousands of hours Michelangelo spent on the Sistine Chapel can't even come close to the thought, effort, and time God put into creating you. Every detail was crafted with intention and love.

I think David sings it best in Psalm 139:

> You formed my innermost being, shaping my delicate inside and my intricate outside,
>> and wove them all together in my mother's womb.
> I thank you, God, for making me so mysteriously complex!
>> Everything you do is marvelously breathtaking.
>> It simply amazes me to think about it!
>> How thoroughly you know me, Lord!
> You even formed every bone in my body
>> when you created me in the secret place;
>> carefully, skillfully you shaped me from nothing
>> to something.
> You saw who you created me to be before I became me!
>> Before I'd ever seen the light of day,
>> the number of days you planned for me
>> were already recorded in your book.
> Every single moment you are thinking of me!
>> How precious and wonderful to consider
>> that you cherish me constantly in your every thought!
> O God, your desires toward me are more

> than the grains of sand on every shore!
> When I awake each morning, you're still with me.
> (Ps. 139:13–18 TPT)

David understood the love of God. He understood that God created us in complexity, that he has a plan for our lives and that we are always on his mind. Feeling known and loved in such a personal way helped David comprehend his worth and praise the One who made him so. God didn't limit his handiwork to David; these verses communicate how God sees me and how he sees you.

There is nothing accidental about your looks or your life. You are not a bargain-bin gal. You were created by the One who came up with the idea of a masterpiece. Would someone who didn't think you were worthy spend all this effort on you? Create you? Plan your life? Give you gifts and talents? Constantly think of you? No. You are worthy.

There is tension between Jesus's sacrifice and us feeling worthy. No, we're not perfect yet. Yes, we needed Jesus to come and save us. But he did so because he deemed us worthy. In Scripture, we see that even before the foundation of the world, God planned this. "Even before he made the world, God loved us and chose us in Christ to be holy and without fault in his eyes" (Eph. 1:4 NLT). So let's settle that once and for all. He called you worthy. You are worthy. We've taken this idea of being "not worthy" too far. Nothing makes you unworthy. Your existence and that fact that you are treasured by God makes you worthy, no matter what.

- Old script: *I will never be enough.* **New script:** *God called me worthy enough to send his Son to die for me* (John 3:16).

- **Old script:** *There is nothing special about me.* **New script:** *The God who created this world loves me immensely and calls me a daughter of a King* (2 Cor. 6:18).
- **Old script:** *My life doesn't matter.* **New script:** *God says that I am his masterpiece and that he had a plan for my life before I came to be* (Eph. 2:10).
- **Old script:** *I am worthless.* **New script:** *God says that I am his beloved child. I am worthy of his inheritance and treasures because I am his true child* (Rom. 8:16–17).

Grab a Mirror

See the girl staring back at you. Take a second to take her in, all of her. Thank her, tell her you're proud of how far she's come, tell her that you believe in her, tell her that she's worth it, and, bestie, tell her that you love her. It may seem fake at first, something you do in the moment, but over time, you'll believe it.

Ask God

Take a second and ask God a question: *What is your favorite thing about me?* Then just listen. Do you know that God is excited about you? You aren't a disappointment to him; you aren't someone he just deals with. No, you are his prized treasure. I've noticed that often the thing I'm most insecure about or try to downplay is the thing that he brings to my mind. It's almost like a reminder: *Hey, I created you just like this! I love it so much, don't hide!* Stop right now, quiet your mind and heart, and ask God: *What is your favorite thing about me?* Write down what he shows you.

Take Them at Their Word

How do you receive compliments? If you are anything like me, you are an expert dodger and can discredit most kind words spoken in your direction. When it comes to family and close friends, I claim they have an obligation to speak that way. When an acquaintance or someone from a distance praises me, I deflect, assuming they don't know me well enough to say those things. There is never a win or compliment I believe. You too? Try something new, and don't dart, dodge, or disprove their statements. Take them at their word. Yes, it's easy to see the flaws in yourself and believe that your flaws are the truth. Why can you trust compliments? Family and friends know you so well and can call out all the beauty in you. They've traveled the miles with you, done the hard work, and have stuck with you. Praise the Lord! Who better to know and speak the truth over you?! Acquaintances and people at a distance see your positives in passing, online, and at a distance and just want to speak life over you. Whether you agree or not, you've made an impression on them. Let them show you how the world sees you.

Finish the Statement

Conclude your negative script with the words, . . . *but God made me worthy.* If the statement you're believing leaves you feeling worthless, then it isn't the truth. Again, try following the troubling scripts with this refrain: . . . *but God made me worthy.*

On the next page is my prayer for you as this chapter closes. It is a declaration that I hope sticks in your mind, floods your heart, and allows truth to sink in.

Your worth is not negotiable.
No job, no circumstance, no title,
and no man can decide it.
You are worthy just as you are
and just because you are.
You've been designed with master precision by
*a creator who is **mad about you**.*
So much so, that your first breath took his breath away.
You are the definition of worth and value,
and you are more than enough.
Now lift your head high.

CHAPTER 5

Old Script:

I FAIL IN COMPARISON TO OTHERS

A 1984 Oldsmobile Delta 88 Royale found its place in our driveway, on display for all our neighbors to see. It was classic white on the outside and had plush velvet seats, in the perfect shade of crimson red, on the inside. To this day, I have never sat in a more comfortable car. Even now, all these years later, I can still picture myself sliding into the passenger side and buckling up as Grandma lit her cigarette and as Loretta Lynn's singing filled the car: *I'm proud to be a coal miner's daughter.*[1] Boy, did she love Loretta Lynn and Elvis, especially Elvis. That car was something special, the perfect amount of bougie for my grandma.

Rose wasn't a typical grandma, which is something we often found ourselves joking about with her. That idea didn't upset her; she confidently accepted the role. When I was in sixth grade, she moved in with my family; I guess I knew that wasn't how most families in our area lived, but it always seemed normal to us. Previous trips to visit her only gave us a glimpse of who she truly was. But not long after she moved into our house, we began to comprehend we had someone special living with us. Our grandma wasn't known for heartwarming cuddles, baking cookies, or sweet gifts. Instead, she was stubborn, full of sass, and a lover of horror movies. Years of smoking led to Grandma Rose needing an oxygen tank to breathe, but did that stop her from smoking? Nope. Homegirl would try to smoke while wearing her nasal cannula. I told you—feisty and stubborn. Heaven forbid if you got that woman laughing while she was walking. Sputtering out her back end with each step, she sounded like a middle schooler learning to play the trumpet for the first time. She made life interesting, and we loved it.

Before we were old enough to drive, Grandma often helped out and took my sisters and me to our different appointments or events. We'd ride in her Oldsmobile, cruising down the street, windows cracked to let the cigarette smoke escape, as Grandma switched between singing along with the music and giving us her road rage commentary.

One particular day, we left the doctor's office and began to head home. Taking a right out of the office complex and onto the frontage road, Grandma quickly took another left up the ramp onto the highway. But she had entered the ramp meant for exit only. "Grandma, this is the wrong way!" In disbelief and shock, my sister and I yelled for her to stop and turn around. I'm sure it only took a second or two for her to realize the mistake, but to me, it seemed like an eternity. To make matters worse, a car had turned off the highway onto the exit ramp. We were then playing the world's most dangerous game of chicken. I slowly melted in my seat to try to hide from the people staring back at us, sending us hand gestures, and mouthing things I cannot repeat. Grandma, clearly in the wrong but not willing to go down with the ship, yelled right back. Traffic came to a standstill and stayed that way while Grandma spent the better part of five minutes trying to turn her car around. I swear she made a one-hundred-point turn—pull forward, cut the wheel, reverse, cut the wheel, and repeat. Grandma was flustered and in need of a cigarette while I hugged the floorboards and prayed for death to save me. It didn't, and, thankfully, we made it off the exit ramp to, once again, travel in the right direction. Why couldn't we be like *normal* families? The whole way home we laughed and reenacted the whole thing. We wondered what might have happened if she had been driving alone and we hadn't been there to rescue (or yell at) her. Would she have continued driving the wrong way and onto the highway? It would have been a story to make the six o'clock news that night. I can see it now: *Cigarette-wielding granny distracted by honky-tonk country music caught driving down the highway in the wrong direction.* Whew—we saved Grandma from a life of crime. You're welcome, Grandma.

As funny and embarrassing as that story is, I know that panicked and confused feeling she experienced. For most of my life, I've felt like I'm on the highway going the wrong direction, always looking at other people and realizing my life doesn't match theirs, stuck in a struggle of comparison and finding a place to belong. The more I talk with women, it seems the majority can relate to life's sudden turns, aborted plans, and changed directions. Inevitably, these events lead to comparison. Then they constantly find themselves striving to gain the ground they believe they've lost. But it's a losing battle. You'll never win trying to weigh your life against someone else's. This I am sure of.

At twenty-five years old, I had been married for six years, I had four kids, and I drove a minivan nicknamed "the swagger wagon." As much fun as that sounds, I found myself questioning my life's direction. This life didn't fit the one I plastered all over my vision board. Did the memo get lost somewhere? All my friends were either single or just getting started with fun careers. Pictures of their adventures, date nights, and free lives filled my social media feed while I sat at home researching diaper rash cream. They were just now stepping out into the big world; it was still full of possibility for them. I chose to thrust myself into adulthood with the fervor to rival that of my husband eating a bowl of ice cream.

Couples with children around my kids' ages were much older, better established, and rocking their adult lives. They threw fancy parties, dressed their toddlers in name-brand clothing, and had big mortgages, while we rocked hand-me-downs like a boss. I felt so out of place and behind. What did I have to show for my days?! It seemed the only thing that defined me was being an overwhelmed, hot-mess mom. Nobody understood me. Shoot, I had more kids in my midtwenties than most couples have in their entire lives! It's funny now, but when meeting new people, the conversation would almost always end up on the topic of college and what I had studied. My reply was, "I planned to be an actress, but it turns out I was better at popping out children." This was my go-to, *I have talent, but my life took a crazy turn*, self-deprecating answer. How I craved the freedom and dream of having a job like other people my age or looking established and fancy like others in the same life stage as me. I couldn't find my place, I struggled to find my voice, and the comparison left me feeling inferior.

Before I knew it, life became a series of if/then moments. If I could just make it past this season, *then* others would take me seriously. If I could just do these things, *then* I would look like a real adult. If I could get my life together, *then* I wouldn't feel like such a joke. Being stuck in the cycle of if/then only sunk me deeper into a hole. The *if* never ended. After I took a step in what seemed like the right direction, another *then* would find me, eager and ready to show me how I didn't measure up. Lost in this cycle, I couldn't see all the good I had around me right where my feet were. Instead, I could only see the things I felt I was not. I held myself up to impossible standards, and I fought battles trying to "win" over others who had no idea they were competing while I sank further into the negative narrative. *You are a joke. Nobody can relate to you. If only you could look like, act like, be like them. You've messed up and can't seem to get things right.*

It's amazing how easily negative words come to mind while remembering truth seems impossible. In our house, we call the negative statements sticky words, because they hold on for dear life. Once at work, I watched Sam and his friend toss mini squishy animals toward the ceiling. The goal was to be the first to make yours stick. It took a few attempts, but both guys successfully stuck their animals. However, now that they were on the ceiling, we had no way of getting them down. The guys chucked items up to the ceiling tiles hoping to knock down the tiny animals, all to no avail. Those suckers would not budge. For months, we randomly tried to get them down until, finally, one fell. Though it no longer clung to the ceiling, it left an unsightly oily residue in its place, like a marker saying *I will not be forgotten.* Negative scripts are like those sticky animals. They are thrown up in haste, and they are extremely hard to get rid of.

Overlooking the water with a breeze to our backs next to trees among the roots and dirt, I sat with Rebecca, a coaching client turned friend. This was our private escape from the chaos and confusion of the world, a remedy she needed but struggled to grasp. There, tucked away in nature, I walked her through some guided prayer and meditation time while worship music filled the background. It's amazing how clarity comes when you take away distractions and allow God to speak. We weren't created to be in a constant state of busyness and stimulation. Out on the water with the sun peeking through branches kissing our cheeks, God met Rebecca, reminding her of the dream he worked to birth in her and reassuring her of her place in it all.

Rebecca possessed more artistic skills in her pinky than most people do in their entire body. She never tired of finding new ways to express her creativity. Most importantly, she was a brilliant writer. For over a year, Rebecca toyed with the idea of writing a book. Agents and publishers reached out to her through social media because they recognized her brilliance. But each time Rebecca began to work through the process of fleshing out ideas, she'd make it a few weeks and then, in a swirl of overwhelm, halt all progress. Frozen in confusion and stress, she would throw in the towel, and, along with that, the idea of ever publishing her words. After a series of maddening attempts and no visible progress, she reached out to me for help.

Within a few minutes on our call, one thing became clear: this girl had all the words. Her frustrations shot out like a busted fire hydrant as she spilled her guts, nothing left off-limits. Nothing beats open and honest clients, because it shows me they are open and ready to make a change. What's that cliché? *You've got to be sick and tired of being sick and tired.* Rebecca could be the poster woman for this saying. I knew this girl was destined to write a book. Truthfully, she needed to write many books, but she needed to see how and believe she could. That would be the challenge. Because while I could hear the pain and frustration in Rebecca's voice on our first call, I also heard something else: comparison, lots of comparisons. This beautifully unique and incredibly talented woman doubted her place in the writing world because she feared she didn't measure up to what everyone else was doing. All her ideas had been done and done well. Rebecca's struggle was as unoriginal as she feared her ideas were. This thought process is one I hear from women all the time. Rebecca didn't need to quit; she just needed to stop listening to the scripts telling her to give up.

We began meeting often to help her find breakthroughs in the areas where she was blocked, and we put plans together to help Rebecca succeed. Inevitably, not long after we discussed a direction, plan, or idea that excited her, Rebecca would send me a message with another *somebody* doing something similar. This sent her into a toxic negative spiral in which she questioned where she fit in. *So-and-so has already written this. What good do I have to offer? Is this all I can come up with? Where is the thread, and why can't I figure out the direction?* As those scripts began to play in her mind, I could see Rebecca shut down. She couldn't see past what *they* were doing to see how *she* could add value. She was stuck in a cycle of comparing her talents to others, and she was falling short every time.

Throughout our sessions, I'd find myself quoting Ecclesiastes to remind her that there is nothing new. "History merely repeats itself. It has all been done before. Nothing under the sun is truly new" (Eccles. 1:9 NLT).

It would suffice for a day or two, and then she'd find herself stuck in another swirl of defeat, one brought on by comparison. Satan was winning the battle in her mind and distracting her from her purpose. He knew the longer he derailed her from writing, the longer her readers would be held in bondage. She had freedom and hope for people, freedom and hope wrapped in beautiful words and a unique message. But Rebecca was blind to it. Instead, she could only see others racing successfully in front of and beside her. This struggle frustrated her, and she continually apologized. She didn't need to feel sorry, because I could see her place even though she grappled with it. The urge to write a book never subsided, though. With all the confusion and struggle, Rebecca still couldn't let go of the idea. But as each day passed, she felt increasingly more behind, fearing the opportunity to step out into her calling was lost. That's when we changed up our sessions and took to nature. That day, we tackled everything, left nothing unsaid, and powered through an entire day. When Rebecca pulled out of my driveway at the end of our session, I could barely keep my eyes open. At the same time, I couldn't shake the beauty and honesty from our time overlooking the water. Something special happened there; she knew it and I knew it. But was it enough to keep her moving in the right direction? Was it enough to help her silence the negative scripts she was believing? I hoped so, but only time would tell.

Would you believe that on the car ride home Rebecca started to question everything we worked through all day? *Does this idea make sense? What if I'm not heading in the right direction? How can I do it any better than so-and-so? I might as well just give up.* Satan is tricky like that. He sits quietly while others are around to cheer you on, lift you up, and propel you forward. Then, in the silence of your car, with hours alone, he starts to whisper the lies. Soon, you forget all the breakthroughs and sit defeated, wishing that you could measure up.

Each perfectly poised and styled photo square on Instagram reminded another client, Kara, of where she failed, what she didn't look like, and things she needed to complete herself. A fun site meant to connect people around the world now caused her to feel crushed, alone, and lacking. Kara and I loved to meet and chat over coffee. As she twirled the straw through the whipped cream on her iced coffee, Kara shared more of her struggle with social media and how it made her feel. How could this beautiful girl feel so broken and unappealing?

Social media isn't a bad place, and, for the most part, I love it. But as a grown woman, it has, from time to time, led to me feeling awful about my body, talents, and life. Because of that, I can't even imagine how it's affecting young girls. One day, after a devastating conversation with Kara, I searched for answers. One study said 85 percent of teens show a significant decrease in self-esteem after being on social media.[2] Guess what? The percentage of negative effects like loneliness, anxiety, poor self-image, and depression are just as high.[3] This explains how Kara had gotten to such a low point. But she's not the only one. According to the study, over half the population feels this way. I'd bet my life savings (which is all of five dollars) that social media is hurting them all. People picture their lives and try to see if they measure up to what others are posting. Are they thin enough? Pretty enough? On trend according to the newest fashion? If not, how can they fix it?

For Kara, her comparison surfaced most in dealing with body image. *My face is hideous. I weigh too much. No guy will ever like me.* Confronted with all the thin, seemingly perfect women, she found herself stuck listening to scripts claiming she wasn't good enough. Then our conversation took an unexpected turn; she confessed to some serious eating disorders. She explained how eating food made her hate herself. Sometimes, she'd remember all of the other girls she longed to measure up to, and before she knew it, Kara found herself in the bathroom puking. Each trip to the bathroom left her feeling more empty, full of shame, and further from her goal of happiness. Her face fell into her palm as she turned from me and toward the window. After a few seconds of silence, she whispered through her hand, "Why am I not good enough?" Tears filled my eyes as my jaw clenched trying to keep some sense of composure. Oh, how I wanted to climb over the table and hug her, never to let go. She lost herself in the lives of others, and, in trying to be like them, she lost how amazing she was. I knew this feeling all too well. How could I help her see these things? How could we get her out of the comparison trap?

Social media isn't the root. This struggle, the one of comparison, is as old as time. We see it even in Genesis with the story of Rachel and Leah. Jacob, forced to leave his family because he deceived his brother and caused quite a mess, went to live and work with his uncle. As he neared the land of his uncle, he noticed a woman off in the distance. She was one of the most beautiful women he had ever seen. Her name was Rachel, and within a few minutes around her, "Jacob kissed Rachel, and he wept aloud" (Gen. 29:11 NLT). Can you imagine being so smitten with someone that you not only kiss her within a few seconds of meeting her but also are brought to tears from the emotion of it all?

A few months passed, and Jacob had worked his heart out helping his uncle, Laban. One night at dinner, Laban, feeling guilty about all the free labor, asked how he could repay Jacob. They struck a deal. Jacob would work for seven years to have

Rachel's hand in marriage. Time flew by quickly for Jacob as he worked those years. "But his love for her was so strong that it seemed to him but a few days" (Gen. 29:20 NLT). Love is the ultimate motivator. For Jacob, the time didn't dissuade him. Rather, it caused his love to strengthen.

Finally, the day arrived for Jacob and Rachel to be married. I'm sure if it were to take place in modern times, this would be a TLC special where we gawk at floral arrangements, *ooh* over wedding sites, and *ah* over the wedding party's attire. Laban threw a big feast as a celebration, and once everyone was full, drunk, and happy, he snuck Leah in Jacob's tent to seal the marriage deal. *Wink, wink.* Who's Leah? you may be asking. Just Rachel's older sister and one about whom the Bible says, "There was no sparkle in Leah's eyes, but Rachel had a beautiful figure and a lovely face" (Gen. 29:17 NLT). Ouch. There seemed to be nothing fancy or attractive about Leah, but all the adoration was saved for Rachel. Can you imagine being the older sister, the one who is supposed to marry first, but nobody wants to marry you? Apparently, things looked desperately grim because Laban, Leah's father, felt as though he needed to deceive someone into marrying her. My heart breaks for Leah because I'm sure she always found herself vying for attention, craving affection, and constantly competing and comparing herself with her younger sister.

I have two younger sisters, and sometimes it's hard to not find myself in comparison with them. I've been where Leah was. My younger sister was the pretty one, not me. She was born on my first birthday and was a constant source of comparison and competition. While we joke about it now, and while I love having a birthday buddy, there were seasons when it crushed me to feel like I needed to measure up to her. Or worse, when others chose her, the pretty one, over me, the ugly but funny one. Growing up in school, there were always the pretty girls, the smart girls, and the athletic girls. Sometimes you found a type of girl who was both pretty *and* something else. Those were the "Rachels." Dang those girls. Quickly, I decided to be the funny girl. Because if I was the funny girl, I'd be able to make fun of myself before anyone else ever could. That part came easy for me. I laughed my way through years of awkwardness, including high school and into adulthood, until all I was left with were fragile, broken pieces in a tough but hilarious exterior. I couldn't forget those negative scripts.

I wonder if Leah tried to play the funny girl on the morning after she married Jacob. He woke up to quite the shock, which quickly turned into anger. I'm sure that didn't comfort Leah. I wonder if she, too, tried to crack a joke in hopes of diffusing her pain, maybe with a quick "April fools!" or "Oops, you mean this isn't my tent?" I cringe as I think of how hard that morning had to have been for her, and then to hear her father and new husband argue over Rachel. *Why can't I be pretty like Rachel, wanted like Rachel?* After all of the arguing, Laban agreed to let Jacob marry Rachel if he promised to work for another seven years. The only stipulation: wait until the bridal week passes because, you know, he *just* married the sister.

My heart breaks for those sisters. An undeniable wedge found itself between them, and it only grew into bitterness and resentment. They found themselves in constant comparison and fighting for the love and attention of anyone around them, especially Jacob. The negative scripts Leah believed ran deep. They were probably started by her father, were echoed through her sister, and were even louder through the fact that Jacob never loved her. It's painfully clear when we see Leah strive so hard to bring love and honor to her family by providing Jacob with a son. Each name for her baby boy was cloaked in suffering because, after every name, she longed for love and acceptance. Reuben: "The LORD has noticed my misery, and now my husband will love me" (Gen. 29:32 NLT); Simeon: "The LORD heard that I was unloved and has given me another son" (Gen. 29:33 NLT); Levi: "Surely this time my husband will feel affection for me, since I have given him three sons!" (Gen. 29:34 NLT); Zebulun: "God has given me a good reward. Now my husband will treat me with respect, for I have given him six sons" (Gen. 30:20 NLT). There was such pain and longing to feel loved. Do you see it? Maybe you resonate with how Leah felt when you compare yourself to others, try to live up to their expectations, and constantly chase their approval. These scripts leave you in such pain, feeling lonely and defeated. *Why can I never be good enough? What's wrong with me? Why can't I be like them?*

As I said, I know this pain, too. But here's what I also know: someone did see Leah's plight and cared for her greatly. She didn't need to strive, compete, or even measure up for his affection. That someone was God, and while others left her to the side, forgetting she mattered, he had a special plan for her. She was a part of his great rescue plan to save the whole world. Through Leah came the lineage of Jesus. He picked her especially for the job. What an honor. Just like the Lord saw and cared for Leah, he sees and cares for you. His heart breaks as you listen to negative scripts pressuring you to measure up, compare against, or strive.

Comparison can leave you broken, striving, and wanting for more. Fearful life has passed you by; it makes you believe good things only happen to other people. This is a lie; don't let these painful thoughts stick. There is truth to be found, and it often comes in a whisper. Let God pull you in close and share the truth Paul spoke of in Romans: "For the Holy Spirit makes

God's fatherhood real to us as he whispers into our innermost being, 'You are God's beloved child!'" (Rom. 8:16 TPT). You are his beloved child, and there is no one you need to fight against or compare to for that honor. It's already yours.

Notes

[1] Loretta Lynn, "Coal Miner's Daughter," recorded October 1, 1969, track 1 on *Coal Miner's Daughter*, Bradley's Barn.

[2] "ExpressVPN Survey Reveals the Extent of Gen Z's Social Media Fixation," ExpressVPN, December 1, 2021, https://www.expressvpn.com/blog/gen-z-social-media-survey/?cjdata=MXxOfDB8WXww.

[3] Meg Walters, "Social Media and Youth Mental Health: How to Find Balance after Pandemic Spikes in Use," Healthline, April 26, 2022, https://www.healthline.com/health/mental-health/social-media-and-youth-mental-health-how-to-find-balance-after-pandemic-spikes.

CHAPTER 6

New Script:

I AM NOT HELD HOSTAGE BY COMPARISON

As I sit here in my office, typing away, I'm in my little escape, closed off from the world, oblivious to what happens just outside my door: a child screaming at their sibling, shenanigans wreaking havoc in the living room, all of which I'm clueless about. Still, I'm distracted. It's the reflection on my computer screen; hues of yellow, red, and blue; a ray of sunshine staring back at me, whisking my mind away and back to race day. It still shocks me to say, *I ran the New York City Marathon.* Twenty-six and two-tenths miles—I did it. Never in my life would I dream of such a feat. But here I sit, with a five-foot by seven-foot flag, full of color, and marked with encouragement from people I love to prove my accomplishment. In secret, my best friend bought this flag and passed it around for friends to sign. Then, on race day, she, her husband, and Sam waved it proudly to display their love and support.

My marathon run could easily be one of my favorite days of my life thus far. While that statement may baffle you, this one might resonate: the 26.2 miles seemed scary. Up until the day of my race, I had only run twenty-two miles. Yes, I know, that is still a long distance, but it wasn't the full distance. I feared not completing the race, as well as running at a snail's pace. Both were equally tragic in my eyes. Unfortunately, these weren't the only things weighing on my mind. Our trip to New York City cost a small fortune. Our best friends made the trek as well, losing a day of fun to stand on the side of the road for hours waiting to see me pass by for only a few seconds. To top it off, many friends and family from all over the country planned to dial in and track my progress. The pressure was on to make this race worthy of all the hoopla. My race-day jitters were on steroids and full of caffeine.

My plan for the race was simple: find a pacer with a time a little faster than mine and stick with them. Having trained alone, I figured chasing someone else might help me reach a stretch time goal. If I was going to take part in such a prestigious race, then I needed to make it count. No quitters or slackers allowed.

With the blare of the gun, my racing heat took off on our long journey through all five boroughs of New York. The moment felt monumental, with our first miles crossing over the Verrazzano-Narrows Bridge and looking out at the Statue of Liberty off in the distance. Like a dream playing out in real life, it felt like heaven. But I had to stay focused. Keeping an eye on my pacer, I bobbed and weaved through slower runners like a boss. Crowds lined the streets and created ingenious shenanigans to cheer runners on. However, my attention was elsewhere. The first eight miles flew by with a speed that surprised me. The next few miles were a different story. Each step,

I struggled to keep near my pacer, and the strain of pushing myself to run faster wore on me. I feared that continuing at that pace might kill me. It wouldn't have, but at the time, I didn't know that. At that moment, I had a choice: press on at this impossible pace while hating the entire race, or slow down and run at my own pace. Thankfully, I had the good sense to slow down. Slowly but surely, the pacer kept on ahead and out of sight. I let go of all expectations and pressure and began running the race for myself. It didn't matter how the pacer or the rest of the racers did; the time on the streets of New York was mine, and I planned to enjoy every moment. Never have I felt such freedom as I did in the second half of the course.

Joy filled my face and oozed out of my body with each step, turn, and mile. Strangers cheered for me by name, told me that I was incredible, and assured me that I'd finish. They held up signs with insanely amazing phrases that compelled me to laugh, high-five people, and point in their direction as a sign of solidarity and respect. Their signs displayed messages like, "This is a lot of work for a free banana," "Never trust a fart after mile eighteen," and, "Worst parade ever." The music of DJs and bands filled the streets and begged me to dance and twirl past them, which I did. I fist-pumped my way through water stations and thanked the volunteers for making my dreams come true. Tears filled my eyes when I thought of friends and family tracking my progress all over the country. The fear of meeting their expectations had been replaced with an overwhelming sense of love and support. Then, thinking about my husband and friends navigating a crowded and crazy city to meet me multiple times and scream my name, I couldn't bear it. I felt the Lord say, *All of this is for you; this is your race.* While the streets were full of other runners, it felt as though I was the only one out there. It was magic, I tell you.

Finally, crossing the finish line seemed surreal. *Did that just happen? Did I run twenty-six miles through the dreamiest city in the world? What is this life?* Overtaken with emotion and gratitude, I began to sob. *Brittany ran a freaking marathon.* The time couldn't have mattered any less at that point. I beamed with a sense of pride and accomplishment (I have the pictures to prove it). What an experience.

How often do we get distracted by someone else's race? How often do we try to keep up with all they are doing that we strive to the point of exhaustion, only to be left feeling defeated and inferior? When we live our lives in this manner, we miss everything God has for us in our race. You can't enjoy the things along the way, step into a good and healthy stride, or celebrate the wins. What if you let go of looking to those ahead of you and instead look up at God? There is a mission just for you and your life. I believe God created a mission with you especially in mind. But your mission and race won't look like mine. That's great news. Let go of the pacer, friends.

Not long ago, we discovered that one of our daughters, Paisley, has dyslexia. While testing her, the school found her comprehension to be off the charts, but she struggled to read the words. If you asked Paisley, the words appeared jumbled and moving around, and even some letters shapeshifted into others. It's a challenge for her to figure out and decode the real word at times.

The night we found out about her diagnosis, Sam and I sat her down to share it with her. We were armed with encouraging words, facts, and even famous people she loved that also had the same diagnosis, including Albert Einstein, Jim Carrey, and Walt Disney. Our goal as her parents was to create a positive dialogue around the subject. We didn't want our daughter to feel inferior, different, or shamed about any of this. But we knew that meant we had to show her how special she truly was.

As we discussed this with Paisley, her facial expression shifted from bright and bubbly to guarded and fearful. "Mom, sometimes I feel different and even bad, like I'm not smart enough, strong enough, brave enough. I'm just different from my friends at school," she said. She went on to explain how sometimes she would go into her class at school with a fun hairstyle but that some kids would laugh at her so she'd quickly pull it down and "fix" it. Then, as tears filled her eyes, she added, "Now I'm going to stand out because I can't read. I'm not brave like you, Mom. I can't be like you." Her words shattered my heart. Tears poured down my cheeks and onto my shirt. Then, after a brief moment, I choked back the tears and pulled her in close to my chest.

"Paisley, part of that is true," I said. "Part of that is your mom being brave. I do look different than other people. I have tattoos, piercings, pink hair, and seven kids. In a lot of ways, I stand out, and the cards are stacked against me. But there's another part of me that feels like a mess. I'll look to your dad and question things that I've said or done. Was it okay? Was it weird? But here's the thing: I will never look like everyone else, and the brave part of me is okay with that. When I struggle to feel brave, I check in with people I know and love to keep encouraging me to show up bravely. But God helps me the most to be brave. I just have to be okay with being different. You, honey, were never meant to blend in with everyone else, and you have to be brave enough to realize that. And the moments you struggle, you come to people like your dad and me to remind you of that."

I wanted so desperately for this precious girl to know and see what we all saw. She didn't need to be like everyone else, and she didn't need to fit or measure up to anyone's standards. She just needed to be Paisley. This girl could change the world, but first, she'd need to stop trying to compare herself with others. That night, as we wrapped up our talk with her, her demeanor shifted. What began as fear and anxiety ended with pride and bravery. Paisley understood who she was and where to go when she struggled to remember.

A few days later, Paisley and I were on a walk, just the two of us. It's always fun to get one-on-one time with each kid, and walks with this girl often leave me lacking words. Out of the blue, she turned to me and said, "Mom, do you want to know what my favorite word is? My favorite word is *yet*."

My face perplexed, I asked, "Why is that, honey?"

Her answer stopped me right in my tracks. "Because my teacher has a sign up in our classroom that says, 'Believe in the power of yet,' and I love it so much. When things are hard, you have to remember you may not be the best *yet*, or that this isn't easy *yet*, or that you're not stronger *yet*. But Mom, there's always a yet. You just have to keep trying." Dang. Y'all, she was nine years old, but clearly she was light-years ahead of me on this whole personal growth deal. Every day is a new lesson with this girl, and I've often said I want to be Paisley when I grow up. She loves all people, believes in the good of everyone, and has fierce confidence that God can do anything. Her ability to push through hard things (like dyslexia) and persevere is inspiring. She is unapologetically running her race and doing it her way. I love every bit of it.

Which brings me to you. Run the race marked out for you. Not against anyone, but at your pace, for your people, fueled by your passions. The writer in Hebrews states,

> Therefore, since we are surrounded by such a huge
> crowd of witnesses to the life of faith, let us strip
> off every weight that slows us down, especially the
> sin that so easily trips us up. And let us run with
> endurance the race God has set before us. We do
> this by keeping our eyes on Jesus, the champion who
> initiates and perfects our faith. (Heb. 12:1–2 NLT)

Life is just like a marathon, marked and planned out for each
one of us. Just like with my race, we are also surrounded by and
reminded of those who came before us. People written about in
the Bible, who, through flaws, failures, and lackluster lives, held
onto faith and changed the world. They ran their own races and,
through their examples, coupled with the Word of God, we can,
too. Like Paisley, we need people right beside us, in real time,
ready to cheer us on and lift us up. They can help us flip the
negative comparison script and see our failures and challenges
differently. When we reframe that narrative, those struggles
look more like *yets*. There's always a yet; you just have to keep
trying. (Thank you, Paisley.)

One morning, as our family sat in the dining room eating break-
fast, Sam came over and kissed my forehead. That's our standard
parting practice. It's cute, I know. Then Sam turned to the kids,
waved bye, and headed out the door for work. Before he made
it out of the house, Pippa yelled out to him, "God is awesome
and so are you!" Sam smirked, waved again, and shut the door
behind him. This sentence is a staple in the Estes household.
Usually, it's one spoken over our kids by Sam or myself as they
head out to school, along with a quick addendum added to the

statement: "and make wise choices." However, that day, our littlest one spoke it over us.

Years ago, Sam and I realized something significant. We influence how our kids start their days. School is tough, friendships are hard, and navigating all the dynamics of growing up can be a challenge. But the last thing they hear and how we set them up to tackle the day as they walk away is: *God is awesome.* We hope that they will remember who he is, what he is capable of, and that he's on their side, so that no matter what they face, that truth remains. He is a big God, and he is with them. The second part of the phrase is: *you're awesome, too.* The same God who created the whole world created you. He doesn't make mediocre, unimportant things. No, he creates wonderful masterpieces who are full of special skills, talents, and passions. In light of this truth, we want our children to live big, bold, and bright lives for God, because he thinks they are awesome, too.

Guess what? It's sinking in for them. The words we speak over our children matter. Friends, the scripts we speak over ourselves matter too. So, bestie, I want to say the same to you today, wherever you are: God is awesome, and so are you. Read that again. Maybe you should even write it down on a card and tape it on your mirror as a daily reminder.

And here's the crazy thing. The girl next to you who you always compare yourself to is awesome, too. Let her shine. Let her do her thing so you can do yours. You aren't falling behind or needing to run past her. She is an incredible wonder, just like you. But the longer you find yourself chasing after what she's doing, the further you may be getting from the life, direction, and pace God has in store for you. Let him be awesome in you!

A couple of weeks ago, I had a group of girls over to my house. The morning before they came over, I realized that some of these gals whom I had never met might be fretting over what to wear. The reason I knew this was because I would be, too, if I were in their place. Days prior, when I invited them, I told them the attire was comfy. But you know as well as I do, that means *very* different things for different people. Am I right?! It's silly, but as women, this is something we think about, and I was not about to let these ladies spend the morning in a tizzy trying to strategically pick out the perfect outfit, one they spent forever trying on, accessorizing, and staring at in the mirror but had to appear to be thrown together. You know—the *I woke up like this* look—except you didn't. With that in mind, I sent a picture of myself in leggings and a giant sweatshirt with the following text out to the ladies: "Because we're girls and this is a thing, when I say comfy, I really mean comfy. No need to dress to impress, unless that's how you roll!" I wanted them to know there is never a standard to be around me. Let me squash that comparison game before it starts. Because truthfully, I'm not interested in surface-level constant competition and keeping up appearances. I want messy, authentic people because I'm one of them. What if people felt they had the freedom to show up as themselves—bedhead, sweatshirts, and all? On the good days, bad days, and everything in between? What if they could be real about the messy parts? What if you could do the same? You might just help someone feel seen and give them the freedom to stop competing or comparing.

I have a cool theory. You will shine brighter when you cheer on the girl next to you. It's true. Anytime I'm coaching women and we touch on the comparison struggle, I offer this solution to help them flip the script in their minds. The comparison game doesn't have to be the wedge we create between us and others. Besties, the enemy is lying to us and making us believe in scarcity, not abundance. If we operate in scarcity, then we see those around us as competition fighting on opposing teams instead of companions fighting together. Scarcity says there isn't enough, but abundance says there is more than enough. The comparison game is a trap, and a deadly one at that. It sends you into a frenzy of negative thoughts, letting you believe you don't measure up and don't have your act together. Ultimately, you find yourself trapped and lost in bitterness. Let's just call comparison what it truly is: sin. Yikes. But it's true. In the New Testament, James writes of the effects of sin:

> Temptation comes from our own desires, which entice us and drag us away. These desires give birth to sinful actions. And when sin is allowed to grow, it gives birth to death.
>
> So don't be misled, my dear brothers and sisters. Whatever is good and perfect is a gift coming down to us from God our Father, who created all the lights in the heavens. (James 1:14–17 NLT)

Comparison gives birth to death, and no good can come from it. So, instead of allowing my clients to stay trapped in comparison, we take a new route. We call out the things we see in others, and we thank God that he is a good Father and an excellent gift giver. Because we know he's a loving Father and good gift giver, that means he won't leave us empty-handed. A shift happens in their minds when they begin to see others through this lens, when they let go of scarcity and allow abundance to pour in. Here's how abundance happens through cheering:

- You take your eyes off of yourself and begin supporting a girl doing her thing, running her race, and making a change.
- You show other women how it's done; they don't have to compare either. You lead the way and remind them that we can *all* win.

- You aren't wasting your time and energy plotting and scheming to try and beat the next girl. You'd be surprised at how much creativity is stifled when you chase someone else's life. Creativity is priceless; use it on yourself.
- You aren't full of stress and desperation to figure out what works for her because you've adopted a new motto: *You do you, boo.*
- You realize that you have your special flair to bring to the table, something no one else has. Don't lose sight of this.

Listen, we are better together. I will say this until there isn't any more breath in my lungs. But we can't work together if we continue to compare. Stop looking at "her" and feeling inadequate. You are the girl God chose for such a time as this, to do the work he has just for you—not for some other woman, because she has her own mission! Don't fall for the scripts causing you to compare your life to others.

The struggle inherent in looking around at others and trying to measure up is this: we weren't created to make people our standard. Paul understood this well and even challenged the church in Corinth with this idea: "Oh, don't worry; we wouldn't dare say that we are as wonderful as these other men who tell you how important they are! But they are only comparing themselves with each other, using themselves as the standard of measurement. How ignorant!" (2 Cor. 10:12 NLT). Paul understood the assignment; he didn't live for the approval of others. We can do the same; let's make God our standard. It's not that we are aiming for perfection, but we strive to mimic his example and live out his teaching. He's okay with that—are you? Let's take a hard look at the scripts we speak over ourselves when we compare ourselves to other classmates, working women, married women, unmarried women, etc. What does Jesus want to do with the script that we don't measure up to? With what truth can we counter the script that says we're behind or not exactly where we're meant to be? Let's speak truth over these negative scripts:

- **Old script:** *I will never measure up.* **New script:** *The Holy Spirit inside of me reminds me that I am God's beloved child* (Rom. 8:16).
- **Old script:** *There is no place for me.* **New script:** *God says that I am an integral part of the body of Christ, and not only do I have a place, but I am needed* (1 Cor. 12:12–27).
- **Old script:** *It will never be my turn.* **New script:** *Through God's strength, I can continue doing good and will see the reward if I do not give up* (Gal. 6:9).
- **Old script:** *I can't compete against her.* **New script:** *God has given me all the qualifications I need to run my own race* (2 Cor. 3:4–5).

Play

Your soul was created to play. Did you know that? As we grow older, we learn to take everything seriously, and we turn our talents, skills, and passions into monetary gain. That isn't inherently wrong, but along the way, we forget what it means to just play, to simply create just to create, to play just for the fun of it. We need to find our sense of play again. Try one thing today that brings you back to a state of play. Take the pressure off of yourself. This will help flip the script in your mind that everything needs a success rate, comparison marker, or deadline. Nope, not today. It's all about the play.

Cheer a Sister On

Give a sister a little shout-out. This can start a chain reaction not only in your heart but in the hearts of women all around. If they see you vocal about your support and love for the girl next to you, they will join in, too. Let's reassure them that it's okay to love and cheer each other on. This is huge, and it starts with you. Can you be the change?

Limit Your Intake

Take some time away from social media. Look, I get it—I am a huge fan of most things social media. But I also know that it can lead to an anxious and discontent heart for me. I'm guessing this might be true for you as well. It's extremely easy to see what others are doing, wearing, and creating and then try to hold our lives up to that standard. Comparing our lives to others leaves us feeling lost and less than. Instead of settling for the highs and lows brought on by the social media comparison game, let's be proactive. Take a break and shut it all down. Focus on the people around you. Fun fact: it's hard to know what you're supposedly missing or what you should supposedly be measuring up to when you can't see it.

Lead with Gratitude

My encouragement to you is to start a gratitude journal. My friend shared once about how she keeps a journal by her bed. Each night, she grabs it and writes at least three things she is grateful for. Sometimes the list reads of big wins from the day, while others are simple things. At first, she said coming up with a list challenged her, but as the days passed, it was easier to see things stick out. That's because she flipped the script. Subconsciously, she told her mind, *We're going to look for the good,* and, over time, it became more natural. Throw out the comparison and fill it with gratitude.

Working to break the scripts of comparison may feel daunting and tough. I don't want you to miss your life because you're too busy trying to chase down someone else's. And I definitely don't want you to feel stuck because you struggle to see how you can win in your life. You are never stuck; don't agree with that lie. Don't let those damaging scripts take hold inside your heart. Instead, let's make a move. My friend and mentor Jess Connolly said it best when referring to the idea of feeling stuck and how there's always a move you can make:

> In Jesus' name, you are never stuck. You can go up: praise changes our countenance and lifts our head. You can go low: repentance brings refreshment and changes the atmosphere around us. You can go back: see his faithfulness and count the work of his hand in the past. You can take a step of obedience or faith forward. There's always a move to make, and you're safe in his love—even if you make a mistake.

Do you see that, besties? You are never stuck. You can always look up and worship God, taking your focus off yourself and turning it toward God. Maybe you need to look down; take a second to check your heart and see if there are any areas in which you need to repent. You can look back and see the times in your life when God has shown up and been faithful—if he was faithful then, he can be trusted to be faithful still. And lastly, you can look forward in the future with hope. When you feel thoughts of comparison rise up in your heart, make a move, and flip the script.

Old Script:

I AM BROKEN BY LONELINESS

When I entered kindergarten, I believed that I was hot stuff. I was one of the cool kids now that I could go to school. Oh, how this makes me laugh, because it wasn't but a few years later when I began to dread school. I didn't hate school; it just wasn't fun, and homework felt like the death of my soul. Alas, this cute little six-year-old version of Brittany still loved school; it was magical. Part of the magic came from the daily rides on the bus. It towered over me, with wheels that reached eye level and doors that mysteriously folded open and shut, but most importantly, it was bright and shiny like the sun. Riding the bus solidified my journey into adulthood. First stop: kindergarten; next stop: college.

But the bus and I had a rocky start. Let me explain. I can't be certain of this, but I think the first time I rode the bus was home on the first day of school. My mom ran an at-home daycare and

95

couldn't come pick me up from school. That was fine with me. Remember, I was practically an adult. That afternoon, when I stepped onto the bus and made my way to my seat, I burst with excitement to share with my mom all that had transpired that day. Looking around as we whipped past buildings, other cars, and people strolling along sidewalks, I realized that we were nearing my neighborhood. Time flew by, and, before I knew it, the bus driver stopped and motioned it was time for me to get off. As I skipped off the bus and rounded the front of the vehicle, I waved goodbye to my new best friends. Off the bus I went. It took me a few moments to realize something didn't seem right. I looked around at the gravel parking lot where I stood and saw a long stretch of road trailing in one direction and a giant grassy field connected to a church across the way. I gathered that we hadn't quite reached my house. What's more, my mom was nowhere to be found. Fear struck me as tears welled up in my eyes. The bus driver betrayed me. I was left all alone and doomed.

After a few minutes, I composed myself and decided to walk the rest of the way home. The road in front of me looked familiar, and, if I was correct, it would lead to my neighborhood and house. With one hand having to hold the strap of my back-pack resting on my shoulder and the other gripping my lunch box ready to wield it as a weapon, I took off in the direction of my home. Like Little Red Riding Hood off to her grandmother's house, I marched along the asphalt path on the lookout for sneaky wolves that may try to eat me. Halfway down the road, a car pulled up beside me and stopped. "Honey, I know you don't know me, but I live a few houses down from you; would you like me to drop you off at your home?"

Mustering up all the strength I could manage, with a shaky voice I replied, "My mom said I'm not supposed to ride in the car with strangers." The grip on my lunch box tightened, and I turned away from the lady in the black sedan and continued my journey home. *Not today, wolf. Not today.* What seemed like an eternity later, I spotted my home off in the distance, and I began the sprint of a lifetime. Pounding the pavement with each step, crossing through the grass in our side yard and up to our front door, and arms flailing like Phoebe from *Friends*, I. Made. It. Home. Though the walk probably didn't surpass a mile, I would have bet my little life savings that I had just crossed the entire contiguous United States. Dramatic much? This feat was quite heroic.

When my mom heard me barrel through the door, she came to greet me and ask me about my day. Her eagerness turned to concern when she witnessed the panic on my face. "What's wrong . . . ," but before she could finish the sentence, I started to sob. Everything that I had fought so bravely to keep down while I walked home came bursting out. A glance in her familiar, warm eyes reminded me that I was safe. My mom scooped me up and plopped me down on her lap. My body trembled, and I recounted the events that had just transpired. There had been a mix-up, like a classic scene in a comedy movie. According to my mother, the bus should have dropped me off on the corner of the street, right by my house. With the front door in sight, walking home from that spot would be a piece of cake. I think my mom gave me a slice of cake to ease my troubles. Thankfully, we never had another issue like this again.

Walking home from the bus that day, I felt abandoned, lost, and forced to walk the long road alone. It's crazy to me that even in misunderstandings, mix-ups, and lost connections, we can find ourselves battling loneliness. These are moments that are not intended for harm, but they can create such damage. Then, negative scripts weasel their way in and implant themselves

firmly into our minds. Almost thirty years later, I found myself
walking a path similar to the one I walked in kindergarten.
Somehow in the mix-up, I again felt alone and abandoned.

I held my breath as I walked down the sidewalk toward the
building. My heartbeat throbbed in my head, like a metronome
keeping time for a pianist. You would think I was walking toward
the dentist for a scheduled root canal and not a casual women's
event for the first time. Usually, unfamiliar places and events
wouldn't scare me. Not knowing a single person wouldn't scare
me either. However, as I drew closer to the door, it became
apparent that a lot was riding on this going well. The woman
stepping foot inside the new place was a fragile, hollow shell of
herself. Instead of a grown woman full of cheer and ready for
new things, she resembled the tiny six-year-old who faced the
long, blackened road to home, alone. I had just endured one of
the hardest seasons of my life: losing a job, community, and,
truthfully, my sense of identity. Forced to start over, I didn't
know how or where to begin. But that Sunday at church, a lady
took the stage and shared about an event the women's ministry
team would be putting on for local ladies.

Having previously worked in women's ministry and desperately needing to meet people, I decided to check it out. But
things did not go as planned. Truthfully, I don't know what
I expected to happen. My expectations were low, but when I
opened the door to see a room of only ten or so women, my
heart panicked. Smaller crowds mean there is less of a chance
to hide, and you're forced to jump in and be vulnerable. *Here
we go.* I fumbled through the front table, wrote my name down

at check-in, and created a name tag. It was a small room with a group of women deep in conversation. A few of the women glanced in my direction as they talked, but no one stopped to introduce themselves. As a grown, confident-seeming woman, I shrugged it off and continued on my way to set my things down to claim my seat for later. But before leaving my items and heading toward the cluster of ladies, I reached for my phone as a backup. In case the awkwardness continued, I'd turn my attention to my phone, pretending to be distracted.

Starting over is tough—I knew this. Finding people in a community that appears settled and closed off is excruciating. *This isn't going well. I can't seem to break into any groups and talk,* I texted, updating my husband with a play-by-play. Minutes passed, and I still found myself stuck alone in a corner of a room no bigger than an oversized living room. How did a new lady with pink hair hide in this group of fewer than ten women? My face grew flush, and I felt a lump in my throat as I choked back tears. Unsure of what to do next, I headed to the restroom. In the safety of the metal stall, I began to cry. *I'm hiding in the bathroom. I don't hide in bathrooms. This is madness.* Sam called to encourage me and remind me of how amazing I was. Before we hung up, I told him that I would give it five more minutes, and if nobody talked to me, I'd leave. He agreed. After taking a few deep breaths, wiping away tears, and gathering enough courage, I headed back into the room.

This time, I stood a little closer to a few closed-in circles, toggling between looking like I was listening interestedly to the conversation and then looking on my phone. No one spoke a word to me. I kid you not. Maybe I was invisible? I figuratively waved my white flag in surrender, walked across the room to my things, picked them up, and headed out the door. Passing the ladies on my way out, I put my phone up to my ear and pretended to be in a conversation. Adrenaline pumped through my body because it felt too scandalous to leave. The embarrassment crushed me. Walking out to my car, the tears flowed freely. Like kindergarten Brittany, every fear and insecurity I fought to keep at bay in the room with those women came bursting out. Sitting in the parking lot and smothered in loneliness, I needed this verse in Psalms: "His massive arms are wrapped around you, protecting you. You can run under his covering of majesty and hide. His arms of faithfulness are a shield keeping you from harm" (Ps. 91:4 TPT). My heart cried for God to hold me in his lap like my mom did all of those years ago, reminding me that I was safe and not alone. Those ladies had no idea who I was, nor would they ever. That felt weird.

Processing that night, I can't say that I'm angry with those women. I can't be. Honestly, I wonder how many women have come to an event that I've hosted or attended and felt the same way. Lonely and embarrassed, they hide in the bathroom trying to gain enough courage to try once more. That's unbearable to think about. I never want to live in a moment like that again, and I don't want you to, either. If you've found yourself hiding in bathrooms, corners, or even in your car, trying to gather the courage to try again, I hope you see that you aren't the only one. First, let me say I am sorry. You shouldn't have to hide. Second, you are full of bravery, and I am so proud. You took a step in trying something new and finding people; that is huge. I see you. God sees you, and he has his arms wrapped around you, holding and protecting you right now, even at this moment as we read from Psalm 91. Do you feel him?

Random lunches with Amy became a favorite of mine. We first met at church, and our friendship turned into a time of mentoring. This girl was a bright light of joy and only a few years out of college and into "the real world," as she called it. She had such a future ahead of her, and my favorite thing during our meetups was to see her face light up as she talked about the things she was most passionate about. Recently, her job shifted, and while she welcomed the shift then, now it sucked the life out of her. She found herself stuck in a cubicle, staring at gray felt walls and computer screens. Somehow, this transition took her away from meeting people and creating things. Amy struggled to see how anything she did added value.

To make matters worse, after a long weekend away working with some youths, she received a text from her boyfriend. They had been dating for a few years, and Amy hoped that one day their relationship would lead to marriage. But when he showed up at her house with a grim look on his face, she feared this might not be the case. Her suspicions proved right. He wanted to break up with her. It was him, not her, he explained. It was nothing she had done; he just didn't love her. The words crushed Amy.

"Brittany, the loneliest part of my week is Sunday morning between nine and nine twenty," she said. Before I could take a second to figure out what she meant, she continued, "The walk from my car in the parking lot and into the worship room is brutal. I dread finding my seat in the auditorium." Amy explained that when she stepped into the worship room, her heart raced. She then had a short window of time to scan the rows of seats and crowds of people looking for someone to sit beside. Her built-in seat companion had left her; other close friends had busy jobs keeping them away from the church service. Each week felt like a race to locate someone to sit with and beat the usher. If not, the usher, holding up one finger, would lock eyes with her and point out the single seat he'd found for her, banishing Amy to the isle of misfit toys. "It's like a neon sign flashing over my head," she said. "I am alone."

A fulfilling job, people bustling around her, a beautiful blooming relationship, and a life with purpose all went out the window. All of these changes at once left her feeling alone and isolated. Deep down, she began to believe the script that life had banished her to the isle of misfit toys. She felt confused and unsure of how to navigate this season. I could hear the pain creep out of her voice as she shared so openly and honestly. It's amazing to me how honest women get when they believe you genuinely care. (Because I do.) Most women I coach find themselves stuck in seasons they didn't ask for, wondering what to make of it and how to navigate it. Arriving at this crossroads, they question whether they deserve this confusion and loneliness. The quick answer I always give is this: *You don't deserve loneliness. It's a lie from the enemy.* But I understand how that is hard to comprehend when life runs away from you.

Our lives and days can be interesting. You truly never know what to expect. When your husband works at a church, you often find yourself there prepping and planning at odd hours during the week. Most of the time, we'd make it a family affair and have everyone go to pitch in and spend time together. This particular day proved to be no different. The kids bounced around the church gym, shot baskets, hula-hooped, and raced around, pretending to be superheroes. Sam and I used our precious time while they were preoccupied to set up for the service that weekend. It didn't take us long, and to celebrate our accomplishment, we decided to load up the kids and head out for ice-cream cones.

The kids funneled through bathroom breaks while Sam shut everything down in the gym, and then we all packed into the van. Listening to music blare and the general chaos that comes with a family of nine, we left for our sweet treat. However, as Sam drove out of the parking lot, he noticed some commotion in the side mirror. It was Paisley, pants to her knees, racing toward the van. We forgot Paisley! With a quick pump of the brakes, the van halted. I jumped out of the vehicle and toward Paisley, with my arms wide open ready to catch her. Full of panic and fear, this poor little girl had just been left in a dark and lonely place and then witnessed her family driving off, leaving her behind. Talk about mom guilt—I apologized profusely. Did she want cake? Pizza? A pony? Whatever it was, I would get it for her.

That's how Amy felt. Life was fun, playful, and exciting. But when she least expected it, the story changed. Amy found herself alone in the dark while she watched the people she loved leaving her behind, driving off to their exciting new futures while she regressed.

The struggle of believing you are broken and alone is not a new story to you. It's one that bleeds out across all areas of your life. Through work, your family, and friendships, there's a script that leaves you wanting more but feeling you deserve less— less joy, less community, less value. Statistics show that three out of five people actively feel lonely.[1] According to a poll on Instagram, 72 percent of people I am connected with feel alone. And we wonder why anxiety and depression are so prevalent. This script is not only damaging to your heart and mind, but loneliness can also affect your physical body negatively. Studies liken loneliness to be as damaging as smoking fifteen cigarettes a day. It's more dangerous than obesity.[2] Friends, that is serious information. We long to belong; even our bodies speak to how desperately we need to be seen and known.

My oldest went through a season when he participated in competitive acting at school. "The apple doesn't fall far from the tree," people would reply when they caught wind of the news. I beamed with pride, thinking he wanted to follow in his mother's footsteps. Then I nearly burst the first time he asked me to attend his competitions. He wanted *me*, his mother, to go with him. I must have done something right. The morning of the event, I helped him get prepped and ready, making sure he could put his best and most well-dressed foot forward. Though in rushing out the door, I forgot to grab a coat to combat the December freezing temperatures. It's okay, our excitement propelled us from the car and into the school without the cold touching us.

The morning flew by as my son competed in round after round. It was exhilarating, until we hit the dreaded waiting period. For those of you who are unfamiliar with events such as this, competitors perform and wait to see if they advance to the next round. The waiting period feels like an eternity because you have to juggle different rooms, events, judging times, etc. What do you do while you wait? Sit in the cafeteria, snack on things you've purchased from the concession stands, chat with friends, and try to not lose your mind. However, as a parent, I could hang near but not with my child while he acted a fool along with the other middle schoolers. Like a mama bird hovering over her eggs, that was my job. Close, but not too close.

With time to kill and nowhere to go, I whipped out a book to read and settled into my lunchroom space. Minutes turned into hours, and, before I knew it, a chill started to overtake my body, thanks to the drafty, large room. Listen, I'm naturally a cold person. I can't help it. At my old work office, my desk boasted a blanket and work mittens. Yes, all year round. Coworkers would walk into a meeting in midsummer and find me bundled up as if I were awaiting a snowstorm. So the onset of this chill this early in the day felt bothersome because we had many hours ahead of us, and I dreaded turning into a block of ice. I began to fidget in my seat, and I tucked my arms into my sweatshirt like a child and tied the sleeves together to stop any air from getting in. Before long, my legs were curled up to my chest, head to knees, and my teeth were chattering. To say that I was miserable is an understatement. But I'm pretty sure I successfully embarrassed my son. That's a life mission for my husband and me—just a healthy dose of embarrassment to keep our kids humble.

Sometime after the lunch hour, I began audibly giving myself pep talks. *Brittany, you can do this. There isn't much longer. None of the other kids are cold. You are a grown adult; you can do this.* Finally, I couldn't take it any longer and had to throw in the towel. After touching base with my son, I headed out to the promised land of my Honda with heated seats. There I sat, alone in my car, curled up like an infant in her mama's arms. The cold reached my bones and froze me from the inside from being cold for too long. When that level of chill hits my bones, my brain becomes consumed with getting warm, but nothing seems to help and the cold creates an ache through my body. I knew it would take a straight-up miracle to chip away at the ice. Thankfully, the trusty car heater proved up for the task.

For me, that's what loneliness feels like. You feel it creeping in, like a subtle chill or cool breeze. But before long, it settles into your bones, it commands all of your attention, and it renders you incapable of doing anything. Soon, you find yourself curled up, hoping to find some sense of warmth and human connection.

Sometimes, others in their brokenness hurt you, leave you shattered and exposed, and make you feel like you're left out in the cold, all alone and without anything to warm you. That pain can be unbearable. We are not strangers to pain in our lives, but what I've learned is that we can sit in that pain and continue to shatter, or we can allow God to use it and heal us.

Shy and *reserved* are not words to describe me. Instead, *high-energy* and *outgoing* sound more like it. I'm okay with going against the grain, blazing trails, and marching to the beat of my own drum. Some may look at me like I'm a little crazy, but I've always hoped they know I love Jesus something fierce and want to boast of his goodness. Since a young age, my confidence in who I am in Christ was set, and I knew God had created me so beautifully unique. It's amazing how fast it all came crashing down. I remember that day like it was yesterday. I could feel it in my bones that something was coming. It was like when you look out at the sky before a storm as the dark clouds roll in, the air starts to feel thicker, and all of creation bears down awaiting what is to come. That was me, watching the clouds roll in, feeling the tension thicken, and trying to protect and predict the storm coming. Only, I had no clue what was about to happen, and I certainly wasn't prepared for it.

That Monday's to-do list was simple: decorate the Christmas tree, and get ready for a Christmas party that evening. It was going to be a good day, or at least that's what I told my husband, Sam, when he came home for lunch. "I have to leave now;

someone wants a meeting with me," he said. "Doesn't look good; he seems upset." As he rushed out the door, I asked Sam to update me after he finished his meeting. I spent the next three hours waiting. First, I assumed he had probably gotten busy and had forgotten to update me. Then I grew angry as I waited for his call; but as the three-hour mark hit, my anger turned into fear. *What could be going on? Was Sam in some serious trouble? Why won't he call me?* Finally, the phone rang, breaking the silence, and I hoped it would explain everything. Instead, Sam informed me that we needed to talk, face-to-face, and I should plan to miss the party that night.

Something seemed off, and the anxiety almost made me vomit. As he pulled into the driveway, I met him at the car and climbed in. Inside the car, he began to recount the meeting he had just left. I could never be prepared for what I heard. The topic of discussion? Me. *It was all about me.*

While building relationships, loving on people, and being my crazy self, I caused great trouble. The man my husband met with accused me of being prideful, attention-seeking, and looking to attract followers. The man said I had no respect for my husband or his ministry as a children's pastor and that it appeared I even struggled to submit to him. What's more, moving forward, Sam would need to gain control over me. I would need to be in the background and take my rightful place as a pastor's wife, being silent and simply watching over our kids. But that wasn't all. Sam was also informed that if he was not able to correct me, then his job would be on the line. "Brittany, I'm not finished," he said, and informed me that if I told anyone about this or posted about it on social media, he could be fired as well. "You can't say anything."

My emotions ping-ponged between anger, fear, defeat, and shame. Words so hurtful, condemning, and devastating pierced my heart like a snakebite. As the venom set in and began pulsing through my body, tears filled my eyes. What started as a slow progression of drops quickly formed a puddle in my hands. There was just the two of us in that car, but I felt as though I had been stripped, publicly beaten, and left for everyone to watch as I defeatedly picked up the pieces. I felt sick, humiliated, and raw. At that moment, my very existence seemed wrong. *What could I have done to cause this? Why were our family's stability and livelihood hanging in the balance? What were we going to do? And how could I face those people again?*

I felt so broken and alone. The next few days were spent replaying my conversation with Sam and combing through my life looking for truth in the accusations. *Was this how people saw me?* What once stood as a strong, confident woman now resembled a shriveled-up grape forgotten in the couch cushions collecting lint. Every fiber of my being screamed for me to run to the nearest hole and bury myself in hiding. But I knew I couldn't hide, because while all of this continued behind closed doors, the whole world needed to see something completely different. The weight of it all felt like it might crush me, and being silenced like a dog with a muzzle felt shameful and gross.

The following Sunday, I dreaded going to church. As I stepped into that building, my heart quickened. I felt like my every move was being watched and analyzed while I desperately tried to choke back tears. *Don't say anything, keep a smile on your face, and just keep walking.* I repeated this over and over in my head. While standing in a room full of people ready to worship, I couldn't help but feel alone. Just like Amy, I felt banished to the isle of misfit toys. As the music started, everything that I had fought to keep down came bubbling to the surface until I was flat-out sobbing. With tears flowing down my cheeks, I raised my hands high and cried out to my Father. But the only words I could muster were, *Daddy, I'm hurt. Heal me.* People I knew and trusted hurt me. They downright broke me, and I didn't know what to do.

With this crushing blow, the cold began to settle in. It robbed me of who I was created to be and left me lonelier than I could ever imagine. *You don't deserve to be around people. Do you see the mess you've created? Just hide in your hole.* The enemy hit me where it counted with scripts so painful I believed they must be true. But even in the bitter cold, I couldn't shake this truth: "It is not good for . . . man to be alone" (Gen. 2:18 NLT). From the foundations of the earth, one thing is true: God did not create man to be alone. To believe differently is to believe a lie. And that is what I chose to cling to.

Right now, you may be feeling broken and shattered beyond repair, much like I was. But let me share this with you today: God wants more for you. He has created you to have a beautiful community with people. You shouldn't have to live life broken and alone. People will fail you. And guess what? You will fail them. We are imperfect people. But one thing is for sure: God will never fail us. Let's take the pressure off of people and give it to God. He can handle it, and he can help us find our people. Why don't we start with this first? Hand over our broken pieces to God and believe, like he said in Psalms, that he is big enough to fix them. "He heals the brokenhearted and binds up their wounds" (Ps. 147:3 NIV).

Notes

[1] Susan Perry, "3 in 5 American Adults Report Feeling Lonely, and Younger Adults Feel It the Most, Survey Finds," *MinnPost*, January 31, 2020, https://www.minnpost.com/second-opinion/2020/01/3-in-5-american -adults-report-feeling-lonely-and-younger-adults-feel-it-the-most-survey -finds/#:~:text=Three%20in%20five%20American%20adults,those%20living %20in%20rural%20areas.

[2] Nick Tate, "Loneliness Rivals Obesity, Smoking as Health Risk," WebMD, May 4, 2018, https://www.webmd.com/balance/news/20180504 /loneliness-rivals-obesity-smoking-as-health-risk#:~:text=Loneliness%20 has%20the%20same%20impact,even%20more%20dangerous%20than%20 obesity.&text=The%20survey%2C%20conducted%20by%20the,least%20 some%20of%20the%20time.

CHAPTER 8

New Script:

I AM NEVER ALONE

Writing this chapter on loneliness feels a lot like imposter syndrome because I don't believe myself to be a professional at fighting it. We picked one of the craziest times to uproot our family and move—during a pandemic. The world shut down, and thanks to a new job opportunity, we said, "Let's go!" And right now, two years into our new life and town, my family has never felt so out of place. My children are struggling to find friends, and I can't seem to find my footing in the community, with friends, or even at our church. It's a sticky time for us, to say the least. This issue is new to us. Not the moving part. Sadly, in ministry, we aren't strangers to that. But we've never tried to navigate such a move through a worldwide pandemic that forced us to hide in our homes, alter our lives, and, for some we love, lose them completely. That has been a challenge. So, I am writing this chapter to you from a season of loneliness.

In fact, the top of the page I'm currently typing on has a header branded across it: "LONELINESS SUCKS AND THAT IS ALL I HAVE TO SAY ABOUT THAT." And that feels like the truth to me. But here's what I know: I'm buying into the negative scripts being fed to me by the enemy. *There is something wrong with you. Nobody wants to be your friend. You are hard to love, handle, etc.* You name it, I've heard it in my head. These are lies. I also know that I'm not alone, even when I struggle to feel differently.

Are you sitting here, holding this book, and feeling stuck in a lonely season? I want better for you. I want better for myself. And I can confidently say that God wants more for us as well. Paul writes in the book of Romans to assure the Christians in Rome of one paramount thing: "No power in the sky above or in the earth below—indeed, nothing in all creation will ever be able to separate us from the love of God that is revealed in Christ Jesus" (Rom. 8:39 NLT). Today, we are going to believe that nothing can separate us from God's love, and that means he won't leave us alone. This comforts me, as I hope it does you. This also means that we can work to flip the script in our minds, a script that holds us back from community with others, because we are loved, always and forever, fully and completely. Now, let's get to work.

It's a Thursday night, and I find myself on my hands and knees with a damp towel and a hot iron in hand with a YouTube video tutorial blaring. What am I doing, you may wonder? Burning my fingers. That's what I'm doing. Also, I was trying tirelessly to dissolve red wax from my white carpet. When we moved into this house, I knew the white carpet would prove to be a problem from the start, but what I didn't expect was a game night gone wrong.

We had been playing a rousing game of Throw Throw Burrito, and the cards indicated a duel between my two youngest girls. (Have you heard of this game? It's a favorite at our house.) They lined up, back-to-back, as you do in any good duel. Squishy foam burritos in hand, we counted down from three as they took steps in opposite directions. "One." They spun around and chucked the Mexican cuisine at each other. The goal: hit your competitor before they get you first. Only, one flying burrito went rogue, tossing and turning until it smacked a lit Christmas candle on a table. The force tossed the candle to the ground, and bright red wax flew everywhere. We froze in silence and tried to process the events that had transpired. Wood floors, white walls, and carpet resembled a gruesome crime scene. It's forever known as The Great Candle Massacre of 2021. The view overwhelmed me, and even though I was unclear on how to tackle the mess, I started in a small section and kept moving on.

If you were to ask the kids what surprised them most about this ordeal, they would unanimously say that I kept calm the entire time. And people think miracles don't happen. After we wrapped up cleaning, we were left with a speckled red pattern on the carpet, a faint Jackson Pollock for all to see as they entered our home. In years and homes past, this would have sent my anxiety through the roof. I couldn't imagine inviting people over with such an atrocity. However, in this house and new chapter, it didn't faze me much. The splatter seemed like a fitting symbol for the chaos of our year. Plus, we didn't have people to invite over who could gawk at our mess. We were alone.

Months later, attempting to flip the script on my negative thoughts, I invited some women to my house. I pulled the trigger on the invite before I had a chance to back out. It was a good thing, too. Because that Thursday night, on the floor, ironing my carpet, I regretted putting myself out there. What if I tried to meet people again and it flopped? *Why can't I make friends? Why is this so hard?*

The truth is, even though I know community is vital, I also know it can be hard to build at first. But I also know that anything worth having is hard. It's showing up when you feel like you don't belong. It's putting in the time to open up and be vulnerable. It's getting to know others and their stories. It's not easy, and it's not quick. But it's real, deep, and hard-fought. That is beautiful.

Jordan was living proof of this. She and I became good friends a few years ago. The story is comical. One night, at a women's event I hosted, she came up and introduced herself to me. Jordan explained that she was new to the area but excited for the night and about meeting other ladies. My antenna went up with the term "new to the area" as I scanned the room looking for a buddy to stick her with. Jordan interrupted my search: "I'm not afraid of people, and I love to talk. I'll find my place." Her statement stopped me in my tracks. The confidence she exuded drew me in as she continued. "I'd love to get together sometime and have lunch."

Who was this girl? I wanted to get to know her. Without a second thought, I blurted out, "I would love to meet with you. Just a warning, I am extremely busy and a hot mess. If I don't text you back or need to cancel, please keep trying. I genuinely want to meet with you." Something about her compelled honesty, and I laid it on the line. Looking back, that was a crazy, cringeworthy thing for a leader to say. I admitted I'm high-maintenance and horrible at keeping in touch with people. Then, on top of that, I thrust the responsibility of our relationship onto her, the new girl in town. *Winning.*

I'd love to say that Jordan reached out and we met soon after, but that would be a lie. My statement to Jordan was honest; it was a struggle to get ahold of me and pin down a time to meet. But she didn't give up. I don't know if she craved human connection and if this pushed her to fight for it. Maybe she saw something special in me. Or, the most likely option, Jordan understood the importance of community and friendship. Either way, my friendship with her has been one of the biggest blessings in my life. Jordan is a friend who holds on and won't let go.

Why do people like Jordan seem so few and far between? The answer is simple. We lead such busy, selfish lives. We are focused on ourselves and our agendas. Our homes have gotten bigger, yet our friends have gotten fewer. We prioritize things over human connection. When it comes to community, we expect it to simply drop in our laps. We yearn for the girl we met at church to call us and make things happen. But when she doesn't, we are left deflated and crushed. This pain leads us to believe the negative scripts playing in our minds—*she doesn't like me* or *something's wrong with me.* Swallowing these lies as truth, we find ourselves feeling alone, isolated, devastated, and defeated.

Why do we demand that others pursue us while not assuming any of the responsibility ourselves? Why can't we take the risk and try first? Maybe we get turned down a few times like Jordan did. Maybe not. I'm convinced that true community lies on the other side of your comfort zone. Jordan knew her worth, and there were times when I unintentionally blew her off or missed her calls. But those moments didn't define her.

Instead, she held onto truth and believed that God desired her to find people, and this pushed her to fight for it. You can fight for it too. It's easy to be lost in the crowd, becoming another nameless face. I know this, and I've played that role before. But for all of our sakes, we can't allow this to continue. We need to find people with whom we share our stories, and they need to do the same. We can't continue to listen to the scripts that lead us to believe we are only worth loneliness.

There's a scar on my right hand that I wear as a badge of honor, mainly because I see it as more of an "I survived this" than an honorable action ordeal. We talked about the time I broke my hand breakdancing—you know, the moment that caused me to need surgery, multiple casts, and months of physical therapy? Yes, it's that scar.

The days following my surgery were comical. Most of the time, I was asleep. But when I woke up, I was hungry and ready to socialize. The only problem was that the pain medication kept me in a loopy state, which was not the best position to be in for phone calls, texting, or even social media use. Clueless to my handicap, I'd grab my phone or the nearest one to me and engage in the craziest of conversations. I can't help it, I'm just a social butterfly. One time, I found my phone, which Sam unsuccessfully hid from me, and proceeded to answer a call. The poor unsuspecting lady on the other end had hoped to iron out details for a future speaking engagement with me. She left with more than she bargained for. Thankfully, I can't recall everything we discussed, but I'm fairly certain we debated the superiority of donuts at some point. Sam quickly realized he couldn't leave me unattended.

One Sunday morning, my best friends volunteered to babysit me, a grown adult, while Sam worked at church. They folded laundry, washed my hair, and even painted my nails. I only remember bits and pieces. Apparently, I'd be in the middle of a sentence, and I would then close my eyes and fall asleep. Thankfully, my friends didn't take offense by assuming this was indicative of their conversational skills. Pain meds can make you do and remember the craziest things. But for me, they were also vomit-inducing. Bless it. Getting up and moving around proved futile. Any sudden movements, and I would hurl whatever food I had just eaten. Sometimes, I'd freeze in midstride in hopes of stopping the madness that was about to ensue. When that failed, my friends hustled to grab a bowl and hold it up to my mouth as I lost all dignity, and lunch. What kind of people do that? My girls do, my bowl girls.

To this day, I'm still shocked by their goodness to me. What kind of people do that? My people. We are open about the big stuff, and we talk about the small stuff. They know everything about me, and I know everything about them. It's not always easy or comfortable, but it's necessary. We've lived through health scares, struggles, and more. After one crazy season that threatened to rip us apart but instead solidified our friendship, I had a set of bracelets made with our verse. We're bracelet people, okay? You can hear the stacks that don our wrists jingle from a mile away. We are okay with this. It's our thing. This bracelet, however, is the most special to us. Etched on a charm dangling from the beaded strand is this verse: "A person standing alone can be attacked and defeated, but two can stand back-to-back and conquer. Three are even better, for a triple-braided cord is not easily broken" (Eccles. 4:12 NLT). We claimed this verse as a group of three. In friendship, pairs are easy, but groups of three, they can be difficult, mainly because it's hard to make sure no one feels left out. But with us, it just works; it clicks. This verse stood as a reminder that what we had was special, a gift from God, and we would fight for it. Through thick and thin, these are my people.

We often hear the story from Exodus when Moses commanded God's people to fight the Amalekites. Moses stood atop a hill and watched as God's army fought while he held a staff high above his head. As long as the staff remained lifted, God's army would win. "As long as Moses held up the staff in his hand, the Israelites had the advantage. But whenever he dropped his hand, the Amalekites gained the advantage" (Exod. 17:11 NLT). But soon, Moses's arms got tired. That's when his two right-hand men, Aaron and Hur, stepped in. Seeing the struggle of their leader, mentor, and friend compelled them to action. They each grabbed the arm of Moses and held it up until the battle was won. "Moses' arms soon became so tired he could no longer hold them up. So Aaron and Hur found a stone for him to sit on. Then they stood on each side of Moses, holding up his hands. So his hands held steady until sunset" (Exod. 17:12 NLT). Because of Aaron and Hur, the Israelites won the battle.

Interestingly enough, before this battle, we read about Moses using his staff to perform miracles two other times. First, facing certain death with no way of escape, he stretched his arm and staff out to part the Red Sea and rescued the Israelites from Pharaoh (Exod. 14:16, 21–22). Shortly after, in the wilderness, Moses struck a rock to create a spring of water (Exod. 17:5–7). In both of these cases, Moses could succeed without others. But this time in battle was different; he needed the help of others. He needed his friends to jump in. All alone, he would fail.

What if they simply stood in the back and cheered Moses on? What if they merely grabbed their best set of fig leaf branches and, with killer moves, chanted: *Moses, Moses, he's our man; if he can't do it, no one can!* But they didn't. Thank goodness for that. Scripture doesn't tell us if Moses asked for help or if his buddies were proactive. Either way, they noticed their friend struggling and stepped in. They didn't try to take over, condemn him for his weakness, or seek out their glory. They knew that when he won, they all won.

There are times in my life when I feel like Moses, holding up my staff, trying to balance life and family and all the challenges they bring. It doesn't take long before my arms burn and shake, begging for release. That's when my bowl girls step in. They are my Aaron and Hur. They hold up my arms when I no longer can, so I can win my battles and so God can be glorfied. The best part is, I get to be Aaron and Hur for them, too. Frankly, that's one of the greatest honors of my life.

I recently heard about a study that took place in the 1990s.[1] Now, I'm not the scientific type; things like this aren't my go-to choice of reading materials. But this one struck a chord with me. Let me explain. Scientists created the Biosphere 2 project, three acres enclosed beneath a giant glass and metal dome. They hoped to study the earth's living systems all in one location. During the study, the scientists discovered something surprising. Trees grew rapidly inside the bubble, more so than outside in their original environments. However, they fell over before fully maturing. This baffled the scientists, who took a closer look. After observing the outer layers of bark and root systems, they realized that the lack of wind inside the dome was a problem. It was affecting the overall stress grading of the trees. If you're like me, you have never thought about the stress grading of wood or lumber. But what the scientists found was that ordinary wind helps trees solidly grow and absorb the sun properly. The bubble and "optimal" growing environment handicapped the trees. They could not thrive and grow to their full potential without stress.

We can learn much from this study. It's funny how God's creation can intertwine; things that apply to trees can even find truth in our lives. Hiding in a bubble, alone and safe from others and the outside world, can only help you to a point. It won't be long before you fall over. The stress, struggles, and challenges of life are never pleasant, but they become bearable when we have people to help carry the load. The more we invest in the idea of community, the more we get vulnerable and let others in, and the more we do life together, the deeper and stronger our roots get. These roots matter. We need to build roots down deep with people so that we can withstand the stress and wind of this world. Other people help us fight the harmful narrative that we are alone in our struggles. But we must also grow our roots down deep into the Word of God. Which of these scripts do you need most?

- Old script: *I am broken and all alone.* New script: *God has promised to never fail or abandon me* (Deut. 31:8).
- Old script: *I can't trust anyone.* New script: *Because the Lord forgave me, I can forgive others* (Col. 3:13).
- Old script: *People are bothered by my struggles.* New script: *I am not a bother; God calls for others to share in my burdens* (Gal. 6:2).
- Old script: *My friends and family have rejected me.* New script: *God says that he is a Father to the*

*fatherless and a defender of widows and that he places
the lonely in families. I am loved, fought for, and belong*
(Ps. 68:5–6).

Grab a Hug

This may sound silly, but it's the best thing you can do for your-self. Christy Kane, a clinical mental health counselor, teaches the power of an eight-second hug. Do you know hugs are pow-erful? They are. Technology, including cell phones, is changing the makeup of our brains. It's negatively affecting our moods and overall well-being. One key component in helping combat this is physical touch. When you hug for extended periods, say, for eight seconds, your body relaxes into it and releases the hor-mone oxytocin. Kane states that you need eight eight-second hugs every day.[2] This is proof that human touch and connec-tion are a vital part of our makeup. Try it; put down the book and find a friend to embrace you for eight seconds right now. (I'll wait.)

Find Your People

I understand that this statement feels obvious, but don't tune me out. We are busy people who struggle to prioritize commu-nity. As we have built beautiful, comfortable lives, we've also insulated ourselves from the people around us. We are indepen-dent and proud of it. But I want you to be brave for a second. Is there a person you've met that you'd like to get to know better? Don't wait for them to reach out to you. Call them. It may take a few attempts, but stick with it. What if genuine friendship were just around the corner? (I'm here for you, too. You can find my phone number and email in the back of this book. For real, reach out.)

Get Plugged In

Want to find an easy way to accomplish finding your people? Get plugged into a local church. Don't just show up on Sundays and be a consumer. Dive in, and find a place to connect. There you can serve, be fed by good Bible teaching, and hang around people! Also, I've found that when I take my eyes off of myself and focus on helping someone else, my mood shifts. I see things differently and ultimately discover that I am not alone. I'm a part of one big family. Find your family.

Work Your Rhythms

I've noticed the times I feel the loneliest and most defeated are the times I am not operating in healthy rhythms for myself. I bet this resonates with you, too. But the term *healthy rhythms* has become a buzz phrase, one that everyone says and one that most don't understand how to use or implement. I don't want to complicate it or confuse you, so let me show you what a healthy rhythm looks like for me.

For me, this looks like creating good work/home–life balance with healthy boundaries. Each day, this means waking up before my children, grabbing a cup of coffee, and spending time silent before God. As busy people, we tend to run from silence, but often, it's exactly what we need. Let the Lord speak into your silence. I read my Bible and have worship music constantly playing. A big objective for me is self-care. The Bible says that your body is a temple (1 Cor. 6:19–20)—love it, respect it, and care for it. Last, I move my body. Nothing changes your mood more than getting up and allowing your blood to pump through you. Running is my jam. It calms me, resets my mind, and makes me feel alive. There are days when I feel the loneliness creep in, and the best way I know to combat this feeling is to reset. I may run, nap (I'm pretty sure there is nothing a good nap can't solve), or relax my body.

Take a seat. Rest your arms on your legs, and close your eyes. Focus on slow, deep breaths in and out. Then begin taking inventory of your body. With each body part, from the top of your head to the tips of your toes, release any tension you may be holding on to. Section by section, feel your body give way and relax. This is a game-changer.

Find your people, and don't let loneliness have the final say or be the label you wear. There is a community out there for you. God promises for us to "have life and have it abundantly" (John 10:10 ESV). Believe him, and flip the narrative in your mind. I'm here fighting with and for you.

Let me leave you with this story posted on Facebook from its author, Jen Hatmaker:

> In the wild, when a mama elephant is giving birth, all the other female elephants in the herd back around her in formation. They close ranks so that the delivering mama cannot even be seen in the middle. They stomp and kick up dirt and soil to throw attackers off the scent. . . . They surround the mama and incoming baby in protection, sending a clear signal to predators that if they want to attack their friend while she is vulnerable, they'll have to get through 40 tons of female aggression first.
>
> When the baby elephant is delivered, the sister elephants do two things: they kick sand or dirt over the newborn to protect its fragile skin from the sun, and then they all start trumpeting, a female celebration of new life, of sisterhood, of something beautiful

being born in a harsh, wild world despite enemies and attackers and predators and odds.

Scientists tell us this: They normally take this formation in only two cases—under attack by predators like lions, or during the birth of a new elephant. This is what we do, girls. When our sisters are vulnerable, when they are giving birth to new life, new ideas, new ministries, new spaces, when they are under attack, when they need their people to surround them so they can create, deliver, heal, recover . . . we get in formation. We close ranks and literally have each other's backs. You want to mess with our sis? Come through us first. Good luck.

And when delivery comes, when new life makes its entrance, when healing finally begins, when the night has passed and our sister is ready to rise back up, we sound our trumpets because we saw it through together. We celebrate! We cheer! We raise our glasses and give thanks.

If you are closing ranks around a vulnerable sister, or if your girls have you surrounded while you are tender, this is how we do it. There is no community like a community of women.[3]

Notes

---

[1] Mark Nelson, "Biosphere 2: What Really Happened?" *Dartmouth Alumni Magazine*, May–June 2018, https://dartmouthalumnimagazine .com/articles/biosphere-2-what-really-happened.

[2] Christy Kane, "The Smartphone Generation," TEDx Talks, February 6, 2019, Educational video, 14:36. https://www.youtube.com/watch?v =hNR7JPUo_wA.

[3] Jen Hatmaker, Facebook, July 12, 2017, https://www.facebook.com /jenhatmaker/photos/a.217119135053756/1336383579793967/?type=3.

CHAPTER 9

Old Script:
I AM FULL OF SHAME

ave you ever met a celebrity? I have, and I wish that I could say I played it cool and acted like it was just another day. But no such luck. Do I look like a girl who knows how to play it cool? Not a chance. One time, I attended a concert for one of my favorite Christian recording artists, Jeremy Camp. My college roommates and I were hard-core fangirls, so much so that we paid for meet-and-greet passes before the show. When we arrived at the table to snap a coveted picture with Jeremy, I passed him my guitar strap to sign. Ah, college freshmen and guitars—a rite of passage on Christian college campuses! My heart raced and my palms sweated as I waited for the Sharpie to brand my beautiful, artistic rendition of van Gogh's *The Starry Night* guitar strap. It is a moment engraved in my mind forever, especially the next part. "This is a cool guitar strap; I like it," he said, handing it back over to me. Without a second to process,

I came close to relinquishing the strap back over to him. It was something for him to keep forever; he liked it, right? But my selfish fangirl took over and snatched it from him before the ink could even dry.

"Thank you, it's a van Gogh, you know?" I rattled off these shaky words like a poet back to this celebrity. He chuckled as my sweaty palm clutched my forehead to hide my freshly flushed face. *Did I just say that? What is wrong with me?* It's safe to say that playing it cool while around important people is not my forte. It's even worse when I'm with a celebrity.

Now, my husband isn't a celebrity in the conventional sense. He's a children's pastor at our local church. But to the families, especially the children, he's like a celebrity. If you're asking me, and I know you are, he's one of *the* best. So when I had the opportunity to travel with him to a summer camp with his job, I jumped on it. Getting to see him in action is one of my favorite things. Plus, as a bonus, I played the role of the cool wife. Or I at least attempted to.

To play the part, I brought all of my go-to fashion accessories: big hair, big bags, and gaudy jewelry—I had the "cool wife" title in the bag. One night at camp, after changing into my cute summer dress, I threw my favorite giant tote bag on my shoulder and headed out for our evening sessions. As I followed my husband through the crowd full of children and parents, I noticed many of them looking in our direction. Each person we passed got a wave or a high-five because, let's face it, we were celeb status, or so we thought. That's when I realized some of the kids were pointing and laughing. What could be so funny? It wasn't until I heard a man yell across the crowd that everything clicked. "Miss, your butt is showing!"

Panicked at the accusation hurled out into the crowd of unsuspecting, innocent people, I quickly looked around trying to place where his comments were directed, all while simultaneously reaching down—incognito, of course—to make sure my butt *was*, in fact, covered. However, to my dismay, that was not the case. Mortified, I froze.

Unbeknownst to me, my beautifully big and fashionable tote bag pulled my trendy summer dress up, shall we say, in a less than runway fashion moment. While the sun still shone bright, it had a little competition from a moon as well, if you know what I mean. I thought I was walking through a crowd of well-wishers and adoring fans, but it was more like a crowd gawking after a car wreck. Did they want to see the madness? No. But they couldn't compel themselves to look away. At that moment, I wanted to climb *inside* that beautifully big and fashionable tote bag and die! I was pretty sure the embarrassment would kill me, right then and there. My heart raced and my mind reeled as a lie implanted itself deep down.

You're a joke; you should be ashamed. You can't be taken seriously, especially not as a pastor's wife. In an instant, my body, heart, and intentions became cloaked in shame. Negative scripts are tricky because they are birthed through stories and moments that you would least expect. Shame is one of the biggest culprits. That was a silly, embarrassing moment that my mind translated as shame. Here's what you need to know: Satan is tricky. He has a way of twisting thoughts, ideas, and memories into shameful scripts we read as truth.

Shame is a much too common theme among the women I meet. No matter their age, it's unanimous across the board. These women live their lives completely blocked from what God has for them because they are living in these harmful scripts and cannot see the way out. The stories that led to the lies they believed are too painful to speak. I have seen women create the most intricate disappearing acts, rivaling even the greatest magicians, in efforts to hide the truth. But when it's hidden in the silence, they suffer.

As she was sitting on the floor in my office, cracking jokes about the latest fashion trends I didn't comprehend, I sensed Julie had more to say. She flipped her phone like she was tossing a coin in a coin toss, weighing with each flip whether she would share or hold it in. *Heads I spill the tea, tails I keep it in.* The tension climbed with each turn until I threw my hand over the phone and pinned it to the floor. "Just say it," I said. "Whatever it is, speak it out loud." Her eyes met mine, uncertain of how I knew there was anything to share and fearful of what might come if she did speak up.

"I've messed up so bad," Julie shared, almost as if to reassure me that I didn't want to know.

"It's okay," I said. "No matter what it is, I still love you." We sat there for a minute in silence, eyes locked in on each other until her secret bubbled to the surface.

For months, Julie had been sending sexy selfies and nude pics through Snapchat. That wasn't her original goal for being on the app. The filters were fun, her friends were on it, and wasn't it what all the other kids were doing? But then some guys, most of them she knew, began asking for pictures. At first, she declined. *Were they crazy?* A part of her felt flattered, though. Somebody liked her, someone noticed her. As time passed, she found herself flirting with these guys and laughed off each attempt they tried to get her to send a compromising picture. One day, however, a guy persuaded her to snap a quick photo. He reminded her it would be gone in a second, nobody would know, and it would be fun. If she was honest, the secrecy seemed exciting, and the idea of a guy pursuing her felt nice. So, she did it. Before she knew it, one photo with one guy became multiple photos with multiple guys.

Julie looked away as tears rolled down her cheeks. The weight of guilt and shame crushed her. She was stuck in this loop and couldn't see a way out. If she ever refused to send a photo to one of the guys, he threatened to expose her. The idea of that proved too much for her to bear, she needed to keep him quiet, so the cycle continued. "I can't stop. My life is ruined." I grabbed Julie and held her tight, crying at the weight of what she shared. A bright and beautiful young girl stared into a dark void that she thought was her future. How could an eighteen-year-old feel there was no hope, that she had damaged things beyond repair?

Shame hides in the dark and is locked up where no one can see but is fully capable of keeping you arrested and silent. What if this was the enemy's plan all along? It was and is. Satan works day and night to convince you that it's okay to make the wrong choice. He gives you permission, and, somehow, those choices don't appear that grand, gross, or scary. It's amazing, really. He's patient, deliberate, and shrewd. This has been the story of man since Adam and Eve in the book of Genesis.

The serpent was the shrewdest of all the wild animals the Lord God had made. One day he asked the
woman, "Did God really say you must not eat the fruit
from any of the trees in the garden?"

"Of course we may eat fruit from the trees in the
garden," the woman replied. "It's only the fruit from
the tree in the middle of the garden that we are not

allowed to eat. God said, 'You must not eat it or even touch it; if you do, you will die.'"

"You won't die!" the serpent replied to the woman. "God knows that your eyes will be opened as soon as you eat it, and you will be like God, knowing both good and evil."

The woman was convinced. She saw that the tree was beautiful and its fruit looked delicious, and she wanted the wisdom it would give her. So she took some of the fruit and ate it. Then she gave some to her husband, who was with her, and he ate it, too.
(Gen. 3:1–6 NLT)

With one lie, we are putty in his hands. Then he flips the script on us and feeds us lines of disgust, disappointment, and shame. *How could you? You are the scum of the earth. People will reject you if they find out.* We believe him because we know what right and wrong are. Deep in our guts, we understand our mistakes. However, the shame is Satan's special twist on the truth. He's a professional, and he has practiced since the creation of the world. "At that moment their eyes were opened, and they suddenly felt shame at their nakedness. So they sewed fig leaves together to cover themselves" (Gen. 3:7 NLT). Like Adam and Eve, we let shame take hold, and we cover ourselves to hide the secret.

Do you know what I'm talking about? The shameful secrets you have to keep tucked down deep in your heart, never to see the light of day? It's in the darkness we lose, because that's where Satan has all of the power. If I'm being honest, I know a little about the darkness.

Beep! Beep! Beep!

The sound pulled me from a deep sleep. What was it? Where was the sound coming from? *Is that the neighbor's car? No, maybe mine?* My brain tried to process the information as it flooded in like a busted fire hydrant gushing water. Sam, slightly annoyed to be up at one in the morning, woke up saying, "What's that?"

"Is that our car? It sounds like our alarm!"

"No, it can't be ours; it's not coming from our driveway."

To settle our doubts, we quickly got up and checked the front window in our bedroom. The flashing lights and beeping were disorienting. We couldn't process what we were seeing fast enough. Then, almost in unison, Sam and I realized that it was our van. Someone was trying to steal our van in the middle of the night as we slept. Thankfully, our blaring alarm foiled their plan and awakened us to the scheme.

Sam grabbed his robe, and we rushed out of the house. Panic set in as I opened the door and watched a truck drive off with our van, wind up the hill, and head out the neighborhood. Then, without thinking, in pajamas and socks, bedhead and all, I darted down the walkway in front of my house and ran after the truck. No way were they going to steal our van, not without a fight! Beating a tow truck on foot, in just socks, sounded impossible. But I ran like my life depended on it. As I neared the entrance to our neighborhood, I spotted our vehicle; the thief had parked for a second to adjust something in the front of the van, which I assumed was his effort to silence the alarm. He slammed the door shut and ran to his truck. I caught up to the van right as he began to pull away. I did what any other sane individual would do; I opened the door and jumped in.

My heart pounded in an effort to beat itself out of my chest while I struggled to catch my breath. Unsure of what to do next, I grabbed the seatbelt and buckled myself in as we headed off. Clearly, safety mattered at that moment. What had just happened? This joker was stealing our van. I ran after it and jumped in. Pure insanity. If the guy was stealing our van, he wasn't just going to give it back because I was in it, and he sure as heck wasn't going to let me go, either. To make matters worse, Sam had no idea where I was, and I quickly realized that I had no phone to tell him.

Suddenly, we stopped alongside the road near the woods. Shoot, I didn't think he saw me jump into the van, but maybe he did. Now he was coming to get me. I sat there in the seat, just waiting for him to walk back to the van, and there I'd be, all buckled in, ready to confront him. But that quickly felt like the wrong idea, and I became keenly aware that he had the upper hand and that I was stuck with nothing to defend myself. I rummaged through the front of the van in a panic. We had no gun; we had no weapon at all. Why weren't we gun people?!?! I was screwed. As I flung change around the console, I noticed a spare set of keys and quickly grabbed them. I clinched the keys tightly in my fist, with the ends poking through between each finger. *At least it's something,* I thought, as I snuck back to the bench seats behind the driver's seat and hid. I watched the truck for movement, scanned the windows around me, and peeked out the side mirrors to see what was happening. Finally, after what seemed like forever, the truck took off again. He didn't know I was there; I was safe for now.

My mind was reeling. *What now? What's next? Where is this guy taking me?* We drove further and further away from my house, and the darkness masked any signs of rescue. There were no cars on the road, but I pressed my face against the windows as I climbed between the front seats looking for some-one, anyone. If they could just see me, I'd signal for them to call 911 and the cops could help me. But there was no one. *This would not have happened if we lived in a big city.* Every so often in the distance, I'd spot a car and pray it was Sam, because in my heart, I knew he was out there trying to find me. But as time passed, hope seemed to be lost.

It hit me. *I may never see my husband and kids again. What would happen to them? How would they deal? What would they know about this situation? Would they remember how much I loved them? Gosh, why did I jump in the van? Lord, please save me. Help me get out of this vehicle.* With each passing minute, it became clear that the only way out would be to jump when we stopped at a light. But every light glowed green; I couldn't catch a break. *I just need one red light, dang it.*

Finally, my luck changed. Looking through the side mirror, I could see the light turn red. Knowing when to open the door and jump seemed like an art form, a skill I didn't have and never thought I'd need. Before I could back out of my plan, my hand grasped the handle, threw open the door, and flung my body out and as far away from the wheels as possible. Like a scene from a blockbuster thriller, when the protagonist hurls himself from a runaway car barreling down the road, about to crash, explode, or meet its untimely end. That was my reality. The crash to the ground knocked me out for a split second. As I woke, I reached for my head and spun around to see if the car continued to drive away. *Thank you, God, for saving me.* But now, over twenty miles from home in a questionable part of town, I faced a new strug-gle. *How do I get home?* Without hesitation, my body switched to autopilot, and I ran.

When I listen to women share stories of when they've faced fear or struggle, I tell them to pray and quote Scripture. It's like suiting up for battle and reminding your heart that we, as Christians, are on the winning side. But can I be real with you for a second? All alone, in the middle of the night, and miles away from home, I struggled. Even though I tried to do what I knew and preached for others to do, I came up blank except for one verse that played like a broken record in my head: "Now the Lord is the Spirit, and where the Spirit of the Lord is, there is freedom" (2 Cor. 3:17 NIV). While tears dripped off my face, I chanted this verse with each step I ran. With shaky breaths, I clung to those words as if my life depended on it, because I thought it did. I questioned if God left me alone on those streets. Did he hear my pleas for help, for rescue?

Every few minutes, I scanned my surroundings for help and to make sure the trucker who stole our van wasn't coming back to get me. Each time a wave of fear came over me, I clenched the keys tightly in my fist. One of the times, however, I looked down and noticed a leather oval key ring attached. Well-worn and tattered from years of use, the words stamped on the side were hard to read. But I remembered what it said, no matter how illegible: "For the Lord is the Spirit, and where the Spirit of the Lord is, there is freedom." I chuckled. *Of course.* Thank you, Lord, for this reminder. You *are* here.

Off in the distance, two beams of light shone my way. Could it be? Was a cop car heading my way? My nightmare would soon end; I'd be rescued and home with my husband. A wave of relief rushed over me as my tough exterior melted and the fragile, shaken girl inside began to surface. I didn't need to hold it together any longer, and my body knew it. After I flagged down a cop, I blurted out the first thing that came to mind as the policeman stepped out of his car and flashed a light in my direction. "I'm sorry sir, I don't have a mask on." Even in the throes of a terrifying experience, my first thought was, *I should have grabbed a mask from the van before I jumped*. I kid you not.

After a few minutes of explaining, what I assumed to be my rescue turned out to be an interrogation. "Ma'am, you should never jump in a car you believe to be stolen. Are you sure it wasn't repossessed?" I realized they didn't believe me. I just wanted to be home, to wake up from the nightmare and pretend none of this had ever happened. I felt attacked, like I had done something wrong. I felt full of shame, and I felt broken and beat down on the side of the road at two in the morning.

Finally, they called Sam to come to get me. When he pulled up, I ran to him, and he embraced me. His arms held me tight and secure, almost saying, *You're here, you're home, you're safe*. The moment of relief came to an abrupt halt as the dispatcher spoke over the officer's walkie-talkie. Our van had been located. It had not been stolen, but repossessed. But why? Nothing made sense anymore. In the dark of night, a tow truck came not only to take our vehicle away, but in its place, it left fear and shame.

You are so stupid. You jumped into a car that wasn't even being stolen. You risked your life for nothing. Now you look like a fool because your car was repossessed. Why don't you have your act together—your finances, your character? You're a mess. Why would anyone let you speak into their lives? That's shameful, and you can tell no one.

Hours later, back home, I sat in bed weeping. What just happened? I had no clue. My mind raced and was filled with anger, fear, and disbelief. Physically, my body resembled a crash test dummy, post-crash. It was limp, broken, and full of excruciating reminders of the recent trauma it faced. The worst part was we had to process it alone in silence. I couldn't trust anyone at that moment, including Sam. Our van had just been repossessed. In the early hours of the morning, we were left with more questions than answers. What we would soon come to realize was that while we assumed our van had been paid off months prior, that wasn't the case. Sam even received a celebration email from our lender the month we last paid them. But then, in haste, he deleted the account and missed what came next. As the company cleared our account, they noticed we deferred a couple of payments early on, which added to our balance. We missed that detail and were living in an ignorant paradise.

The next few days were filled with discreet, uncomfortable calls to family asking them to loan us money to free our van from "jail." I couldn't believe we were grown adults with our lives in shambles begging for our parents to come and rescue us. This only added to the crippling shame. We carried the weight in the dark, because how could we admit to anyone what we did? And like that, a deep, painful script was born, one I would dig a hole and hide in forever before admitting the truth to anyone. Satan *is* a snake. He's a boa constrictor out for the kill, watching for the moment he can attack. He wraps you up with a weight and pressure that crushes and suffocates any life out of you.

That night could easily go down in the record books as one of the scariest and craziest nights of my entire life. Still, as I am writing this a year later, some triggers pop up that send my body into a panic. One piece of this story never embarrassed me; I'm not sure how it escaped the grasp of Satan, but it did. When the officers' interrogation turned into condemnation for jumping into a van that I believed was stolen, I defensively retorted. "Well, clearly when it comes to fight or flight, I'm all fight." Sarcastic? Sure. True? Absolutely. In all the madness, I gleaned a valuable lesson. When something is wrongfully taken, your girl will fight to get it back—in that case, a vehicle; in this case, with you, your freedom.

Freedom from secrets can appear scary. I get it; really, I do. But is hiding in shame working out for you? For most of the women I coach, it's not—myself included.

The other night, while Sam and I binge-watched Netflix before bed, I heard a quote from *Call the Midwife*. The words pierced my heart like they were trying to unlock and set free the places I had chained up with my script of shame.

> Secrets can maim us. Shame can close us off. What we bury drags us down, and there can be no flight from it. Speak. Speak up. Speak out. Find the words to express the facts that matter. Bring them out into the light, into the air. Hiding heals nothing. Silence saves no one. When we are heard we can be acknowledged. When we are known we can belong. Bound together we are stronger and braver than we know. Alone we are fragile and at mercy of the storm.[1]

When the secret is given power, we will lose it every time. But what if we speak what we are afraid to utter? What if we bring what is in the darkness into the light? Where there is light, darkness cannot be. It's a simple fact. Walk into a dark room and turn on a flashlight; instantly, the darkness dissipates as far as the powerful ray of light shines. The apostle John referred to Jesus as the light when he wrote, "The light shines in the darkness, and the darkness can never extinguish it" (John 1:5 NLT). How do we win over the darkness of the shame spoken over our hearts? We bring the light of Jesus, and we watch the darkness run.

Note

[1]Afia Nkrumah, dir., *Call the Midwife*, season 10, episode 6. Aired May 23, 2021, on BBC1.

CHAPTER 10

New Script:

I AM NOT ASHAMED

The notification popped up on my phone: "Thank you, God, for this freedom." I smiled at the realization of what the phrase meant. Months prior, I spent time coaching a young lady named Brooke through a difficult season of life. She eagerly jumped at the idea of working with a life coach, but the areas she wished to pursue during our time coaching were less clear. As we began walking through our sessions, I could tell Brooke lived in a state of exhaustion and was overwhelmed. She viewed her marriage and job—really, every aspect of her life—through a lens of survival. We labored hard to reframe thoughts, create action plans, and navigate a way through to a new mindset. Truthfully, it seemed as if we were just spinning in circles. Our conversations continued looping around like a car stuck on a roundabout.

Finally, in an effort to shake things up, I asked her, "What would you do if you could do anything and knew God wouldn't let you fail?" Silence filled the room for a few minutes until Brooke leaned in with a nervous grin on her face and shared her dream. Something she had never spoken of to anyone filled her with validation as each word left her lips. Brooke wanted to open up a rehabilitation center for people seeking a new life and freedom from addictions. Her ideas and insights burned with passion, a passion that came from her deep, dark secret.

Years ago, Brooke found herself in a pit of despair with her own drug addiction. In her lowest moment, she came close to ending her life. Through the help of the Lord, good people, and a facility, much like the one she dreamed about, Brooke made it to the other side. Her story left me speechless. I didn't know that version of Brooke, and that was intentional on her part. The years wasted on drugs and the struggles that came with it still haunted and filled her with shame. She beat herself up over who she used to be, a person she no longer knew but couldn't get away from. Instead of allowing scripts of redemption and beauty to fill the cracks the Lord had restored, Brooke tried to hide the broken pieces in the dark recesses of her heart, thinking that if she buried them deep enough, they might just go away. Until then, she'd play the role of a nice and tidy Christian woman, the one others knew and expected her to be. But the weight of this facade crushed her.

My heart broke; this couldn't be the end of her story. She was stuck living a life just to cover the shame of her previous choices. I knew God wouldn't free her from the chains of her past just to lock her up in the shame of silence. Brooke's dreams were purposefully beautiful, and God wanted to use this story from her past to help others. Her past equipped her in such a way to know exactly what and how to help others find freedom.

But it needed to start with her bringing her story to the light, to find safe people to share these pieces of her past with. Like John reminds us, "They overcame him by the blood of the Lamb and by the word of their testimony" (Rev. 12:11 NKJV). Her story, her past, no matter how painful, could be used to remind others they are not alone. She could hold the keys to their future. *That* was power and nothing to be ashamed of. That was the truth I called up and out of her. As we walked through the rest of our sessions together, we focused on ways to rewrite the negative scripts in her heart, and she created a document in the notes section on her phone. Without me asking, Brooke shared her list with me, and each time she added a sentence to the note and rewrote those negative scripts, my heart burst with pride. This girl was the definition of brave.

> Thank you, God, for this freedom! I am going to change the world! The devil is a liar. God can and will use this for my good and for his glory! One step at a time. It will get harder before it gets better. This is a new beginning. Full of hope and joy and lessons. It is exciting. I am so thankful. God, please, show me the way. What is next? I'll do and go where you send me. I want to heal and walk with you, I want you to be my provider and protector. I am strong. The closer I get to God's purpose for me the more I will be attacked, especially where it hurts. And that's okay. Because my God is greater! And the battle has already been won! Hallelujah!

That broken, fragile girl no longer existed, and a beautifully redeemed one stood in her place. A switch flipped in her life when she called out the scary, dark parts. She recognized the lies of the enemy, who planted such hurtful and damaging scripts. She then brought them to light and shined truth on them, which led to her bravely stepping out into freedom. Her freedom from shame is contagious. Shelley Giglio, a women's pastor at Passion City Church in Georgia, once wrote on Instagram, "It's very hard to tame a free woman," and I couldn't agree more. There's no taming Brooke; she is free and on a mission. This is my prayer for you, too—that you would call out the shame you hide and bring it to light, allowing God, his Word, and safe friends to help you change the harmful scripts that you believe. Maybe even right now, at this moment, could you be brave enough to believe that God can heal you and make you free? Could you speak this out loud in faith? I'll do it with you: *Thank God for this freedom!*

You see, like Brooke, I too have been broken in so many pieces that I began to question whether God just needed to throw me away. *What good was I anymore?* In the dark and shameful places, those are the words that scream the loudest. Because our flaws are fatal, right? That's what our society teaches us. If it's broken, throw it away and replace it with something new. We load the curbs with broken, discarded junk on trash days—cracked chairs, shattered dishes, and unrepaired toys all ready to meet the green truck of doom because the owner decided they no longer had value. It's the proverbial hall of shame for every neighborhood.

Have you seen *Toy Story 3*? You might want to go ahead and grab a tissue. Near the end of the third movie in the franchise, Woody and his gang find themselves in a garbage dump where they narrowly escape toy doom a few times. Each time, relief meets their faces as they believe the battle is done, until the next round comes. Finally, they see a light. But to their dismay, this isn't the light to freedom; it's the light of a fiery incinerator. The toys begin scaling the trash heap and try to move further and further away from the flames, which proves unsuccessful. Jessie essentially yells out, *Buzz, what are we going to do?* Seeing the terror in Jessie's face, Buzz gathers his thoughts and silently reaches for her hand. They know the time has come. One by one, each toy grabs the other's hand, and the scene ends with a deep and crushing moment as Buzz and Woody lock eyes. The music swells as the toys tearfully clench their eyes and cling to their friends. The end is near, and they accept their fate. I watched the movie when it first came out, and the theater filled with sniffles, "oh no's," and shock as an animated children's movie brought us to tears. (You may never throw anything away again after this.)

Do you know that broken and shattered feeling? You've just assumed the trash is the best place for you. You've accepted your fate. But this doesn't have to be your future. The amazing news is that God sees us differently. He loves to take us, broken hearts and all, and make them whole. Just like in the movie, a last-second escape can be yours if you are willing to let those cracks show.

I once read about a pottery process developed in Japan over four hundred years ago. It's called *kintsugi*, the art of embracing damage. These artists take broken ceramic pieces, restore them, and seal them back together. But instead of hiding the cracks or flaws, they trace them with brilliantly shining gold paint to highlight their mended parts. After all is said and done, those once dump-worthy pieces of pottery are now stronger and worth way more money than when they were first created.

143

The same can be said about God; he is the ultimate *kintsugi* artist. He sent his Son, Jesus, into a dump-worthy world to redeem and restore us. Because of this, we don't have to live alone, unequipped, or broken. Instead, he wants to take those hard places, those broken pieces, all those sins, and restore us and let us shine so we will be worth so much more than we ever were before.

Let me ask you again. Are you broken? Are you hiding in the shameful scripts you believe? Look around at the broken pieces of your heart, and slowly pick up each dark sliver and hold it up to the brilliance of his light. Because, friend, you need to see some truth outshine that shame, truth about who God is and who you are in him, knowing that only "In Your light we see light" (Ps. 36:9 NKJV). It will possibly be one of the hardest, bravest things you've ever done, but you are worth it. Also—can I just say this?—there is beauty in you and in your brokenness, not later when you're "fixed" or after your life moves on and things get better, but right now, in the brokenness, there is beauty. You are worthy of love, right here, right now.

A huge part of overcoming the script of shame is learning to find biblical hope. God is the ultimate hope giver and turns everything painful into something beautiful if you're willing to be a part of it. Speaking of pain, try being Israel, a nation chosen by God, stuck in exile, and captive to the Babylonians, a group of people known for their harsh ways and ungodly behavior. The Jews struggled to follow and obey God. Many attempts were made to convince the people of God to turn away from the sin they were in and return, but to no avail.

Sometimes we find ourselves in an exile of our own because of the choices we've made. Before you know it, all hope appears lost and your future is grim. That was the Jewish people. The prophet Jeremiah called out to the Jews while they were in exile, and boy, did he say a lot, but not many listened. Frankly, Jeremiah was one of the most unsuccessful prophets, according to the world's standards. People didn't listen to him, others fought against him, he didn't have any wealth, and, by most of the world's criteria, he flopped. But that's not how things are measured in the kingdom of God. Jeremiah had a job to do— speak truth to God's people—and that's exactly what he did. He met people in the midst of struggle and loss, and he wanted desperately for them to heed God's words and find hope. He was a good man.

Jeremiah 29:11 says, "'For I know the plans I have for you,' declares the LORD, 'plans to prosper you and not to harm you, plans to give you hope and a future'" (NIV). Most people stop at the end of this verse, assuming their life will be wrapped up in a neat little bow. I mean, it does make a great decorative sign or pillow, but I'm afraid we miss the point in this passage if we do so. There is power when we keep reading. Looking a bit further, it says,

> "Then you will call on me and come and pray to me, and I will listen to you. You will seek me and find me when you seek me with all your heart. I will be found by you," declares the LORD, "and will bring you back from captivity. I will gather you from all the nations and places where I have banished you," declares the LORD, "and will bring you back to the place from which I carried you into exile." (Jer. 29:12–14 NIV)

These people were broken, lost in exile, and needed hope. And the Lord said, *This is how you'll get it. Call on me, seek me with your whole heart, and I will bring you back. I will restore those cracks.*

Can I echo the prophet Jeremiah for a second? Come to the Father. He is calling you, showing you what you need to do and how to heal, and reminding you that he has a beautiful plan for your life. Your past, no matter how painful, can truly be one of your biggest gifts for the future. Your story can help shine the light for the person next to you who may find themselves shattered in pieces of their own. Not long ago, I heard this quote from well-known pastor and author Bill Johnson, and it plays in my mind as negative scripts try to take hold. I think you need it too, bestie. "Any area of my life for which I have no hope is under the influence of a lie."[1] Try trading your old scripts, which lack hope, for new ones:

- **Old script:** *I am ashamed of my mistakes.* **New script:** *Because of what Jesus did for me, I know there is no condemnation for those who are in Christ* (Rom. 8:1–2).
- **Old script:** *Because of my past, God can't use me.* **New script:** *God promises to help me to do his will and not live in disgrace* (Isa. 50:7).
- **Old script:** *I have done wrong; therefore, I am wrong.* **New script:** *I am a fully accepted and beloved child of God* (Rom. 8:15–16).
- **Old script:** *I am a broken mess.* **New script:** *God is doing a good work in me and is faithful to continue working in and with me* (Phil. 1:6).

Love is the biggest and best way to fight shame and flip the script. Nothing spells out love like the truth of God's Word. As you work through these new scripts, speak them over your life, and walk them out each day, I need you to remember the biggest factor fighting against your freedom—the desire to hide. Shame grows in secrecy, silence, and the fear of judgment. It can hold you hostage while taking your life and your potential for ransom. But it doesn't have to. Satan wants you to live in that shame, but Jesus wants so much more for you. Fighting shame takes some work, vulnerability, and being honest with where you're at. The following are a few practical ways for you to break the silence and begin to shift your thinking.

Find the Chair

When you notice negative thoughts, feelings, or even tensions rise up in your body, you need to stop and listen. Let me use this analogy to explain. Your life is a table, and each chair at the table is a different piece of you—a little girl, a curious teen, a young mom, etc. Each seat holds different seasons of life, including struggles, trauma, and so on. But each chair is worthy and valid, and each chair needs a spot at your table. It's all part of your story. But often, when one version of you finds herself standing and screaming in her chair, crying out to be noticed, you don't pay attention or give her notice. We shut her up, trying to silence and hide what is really going on. Instead, why don't we recognize her, see what she says, where she's been triggered, and perhaps even the harmful script she's believing. Only then can she be helped. (Shoutout to a friend for this analogy.) One of my dearest friends once told me that her younger self needed a hug and to know she wasn't alone. You better believe I grabbed and pulled her in tight and whispered the truth to her lies.

Share Your Story; Be Real and Honest

When you speak, others feel seen and understand that they aren't the only ones struggling. Giving it words will help you awaken and leave the shame behind. Trust me—when you share your story in safe places, fear, guilt, and shame lose power. How do you find safe places? Find a few people who you think might fit the bill, and then try it out with small things. If it goes well, great. Open up more. If it tanks horribly, I'm sorry, but I need you to be brave and try again. Your people are out there, and they are ready and waiting to help you flip the script on shame.

Listen and Love

If you have been trusted with someone's story, don't try to fix the problem, and don't share your growth points or anything of the sort. Just sit and love. Let the person sharing feel like they belong and are beautiful, in that moment, as they are. (Because they are.) They aren't beautiful *when* things are fixed; they are so incredibly loved right then and there. They are an image bearer of God. Show them that.

Shine a Light

Don't hide behind mistakes or toxic scripts. The secrecy causes you to become trapped even further. Speak the truth, and shine a light in the darkness. The light I'm speaking of is God. What does his Word say? Are there things you need to confess and get off your chest? Drop the weight, and cling onto forgiveness. There is freedom and hope in Christ Jesus. It's yours for the taking. Now grab a friend to speak this over you, or let me speak it: "Therefore, there is now no condemnation for those who are in Christ Jesus" (Rom. 8:1 NIV).

You can take these steps to walk in freedom. It's time to drop the shame, bestie. Speak up, because your life is worth it. Let me leave you with this truth written by David as he praised God in the book of Psalms: "You've gone into my future to prepare the way, and in kindness you follow behind me to spare me from the harm of my past. You have laid your hand on me!" (Ps. 139:5 TPT). Take heart, the Lord has gone ahead and prepared a way for your future. It's not ruined, it's not over, there is still hope. At the same time, he follows behind you to protect you from the harm of your past. You have the freedom to move forward, without shame, without hiding, without hesitation. Let him redeem the negative scripts that broke you.

Note

---

[1] Bill Johnson, Facebook post, December 27, 2011, https://www .facebook.com/BillJohnsonMinistries/posts/any-area-of-my-life-for-which -i-have-no-hope-is-under-the-influence-of-a-lie/10150449411323387/.

CHAPTER 11

Overall Script:

I CAN SHINE

March 2020. Reading those words probably brings on a visceral reaction. You cringe, grimace, and remember how life completely changed in what seemed like an instant. Two words, yet they speak volumes. It reminds me of when someone references 9/11; there's an understanding that those numbers refer to the terrorist attacks on the United States on September 11, 2001. More importantly, if you're old enough, your mind automatically transports you back to the moment you knew what was transpiring that day. It's a crazy phenomenon, and it reminds me of how truly incredible our brains are. The words *March 2020* cause a similar reaction for me.

Weeks prior to March, the media buzzed with a new virus sweeping the world: COVID-19. The information proved slim, and because of this, panic grew. At around that time, I had a speaking event out of state and would need to fly from our home in Houston to New Orleans, Louisiana. As the day of my departure approached, word spread of events, gatherings, and even stores shutting down in an effort to stop the spread of the virus. My event, however, remained good to go, and I jumped on a flight and felt excited to escape the chaos as a mom of seven and speak to ladies about their worth. The next moment is seared into my brain forever. When our plane landed, I grabbed my phone and turned it on, like I always do. But before I had a chance to let my family know I made it safely in Louisiana, my phone dinged with notification after notification. The governor of Louisiana planned to shut down the entire state. I panicked. The world greatly changed in such a short time while I remained blissfully unaware in the sky. A message from the event coordinator was among the list of the notifications I missed. She let me know they still planned to meet, but she understood if I desired to cancel. I'm all about making lemonade from lemons, plus I *did* just land in her state, so I planned to make the best of it. She couldn't keep me away.

After speaking to a mostly empty room of ladies, I set off to the airport, ready to head home. Stepping into the airport, my eyes scanned my surroundings and were unsure of what they saw. A building that normally appeared to be crowded with people bustling around seemed like a ghost town. Not only were the people missing, but the ones who remained lacked joy. Something reached in and sucked out every bit of joy and replaced it with worry. The oddities didn't stop with the smaller crowds. Some of the people present were wearing face masks. It's funny to look back on this because the idea of face masks no longer seems odd. But that day, those who wore them felt extreme to me. Clearly, I had no clue what was about to happen.

Only five people were passengers on the plane that day. Our precious flight attendants scrambled to keep the passengers at ease, and they gave us all the complimentary food and drinks we desired. We toasted to whatever may come, and we cracked jokes about our "packed" flight and swapped life stories. Before long, the cabin grew quiet as the weight of what would greet us at home hit us. My gaze turned to the window. Staring out at an open sky full of light and fluffy clouds felt peaceful. Each color, hues of blue, yellow, and orange, perfectly blended into the next. The clouds danced across the sky as if they moved to a beautiful melody. My mind wandered to Psalm 19:1, and I believed that David must have written it in a moment like this: "The heavens declare the glory of God; the skies proclaim the work of his hands" (NIV). God's glory, displayed for all to see. For the next two hours, I was gifted an escape from reality. But in the escape, I met the glory of God. His presence comforted and reminded me that I could trust the work of his hand. I didn't know how much life would change or how this moment would be the beginning of the end, the end of life as we knew it. If I had known the significance it held, I might have cherished it a little longer; I might have tried to soak in a few more seconds of his glory as it shone over our plane.

As time passes, the beauty of that memory increases. It's true that it was one of the hardest seasons I have walked through. When I recount the events and circumstances that are the hardest I have ever faced, something else stands out. In those seasons, there have been "glory moments," little pockets of memories when I could nearly feel the tangible presence of God on me, like a ray of sun shining down and kissing me on the cheeks—so personal and precious, but compelling me to continue on and, in turn, shine for others to see. Do you have "glory moments," too?

Moses sure did. In the book of Exodus, Moses was tasked with the job of leading the Hebrew people to the promised land. This came on the heels of their newfound freedom from Pharaoh and the Egyptians. But before Moses made any big moves, he wanted to make sure the Lord would go with him. He knew the Lord's favor and presence was the only way they could make it. After a back and forth between Moses and God, Moses asked for God to show his glory to him. There, on top of Mount Sinai, God tucked Moses in the cleft of a rock and passed in front of him, allowing Moses to get a glimpse of God's glory. Immediately, Moses dropped to his knees and worshiped God. For the next forty days, he stayed on top of the mountain with the Lord. When Moses came down the mountain after receiving the Ten Commandments, the Bible says he was literally shining: "He wasn't aware that his face had become radiant because he had spoken to the LORD" (Exod. 34:29 NLT). He spent time with God, and he glowed because of it.

Now, it's easy to see this beautiful moment between God and Moses and forget all of the others that brought him to that encounter. His story is similar to ours. Did he have wonderful glory moments? Yes. But he also faced struggles, struggles much like you and I have been working through in this book. Let me walk you through them for a second.

Failure and Shame

The book of Exodus opens with fear. Pharaoh feared the Hebrew people who grew in numbers and, in his mind, threatened his reign. His fear forced him to turn God's chosen people into slaves while also instructing his people to kill all newborn baby boys. Moses was born during this strong Egyptian oppression, and Moses's mother feared for his life and hid him in a basket, which she placed, with Moses inside, in the Nile River. I cannot imagine the desperation of his mother, but her bravery allowed God to work. In the Nile one day, an Egyptian princess found the baby and ultimately rescued him and adopted him into her family. As Moses grew, he found himself caught between two worlds: one of Egyptian royalty, and the other of an enslaved Hebrew people. The tension came to a head one day when Moses witnessed the cruel beatings and hard work his people were forced to do. In the heat of passion, Moses killed an Egyptian and then quickly tried to hide his body in the sand. But like I tell my children, the truth will always surface, no matter how deep you bury it. Sure enough, the same is true in this story. "Then Moses was afraid, thinking, 'Everyone knows what I did'" (Exod. 2:14 NLT). His life now in danger for a second time, Moses fled the land.

I don't know about you, but I'd say that killing a man would qualify as a failure. This is no *Oops, I ran a red light*. It's murder. In feeling shame from his mistake, Moses did the only thing he knew to do: run. He ran from the consequences, he ran from the people he had failed, and he ran to hide in isolation. Sound familiar? We have all sat in the aftermath of our failures and hid in shame. But the thing I want you to see here is not the mess; it's what comes next. That wasn't the end of Moses' story. Actually, it was the beginning. God didn't look down at him and think, *Why did I save your life as a baby for you to ruin it at such a young age?* Quite the opposite, my friends. God turned Moses's failures and shame into something that he would ultimately get the glory for. Just like with Moses, your mistakes don't have to be the end.

Worth and Comparison

Years later on a mountainside, Moses heard a plan from God, and it was a crazy one. God spoke to him through a burning bush. Honestly, if I heard the voice of God come from a blazing piece of shrubbery, I'd freak. Moses didn't bat an eyelash. Instead, he stepped closer and talked to God. What a guy. The time had come for God to send rescue to his people, and he wanted to use Moses to lead the way. But Moses questioned God by highlighting all of his shortcomings. "But Moses pleaded with the LORD, 'O Lord, I'm not very good with words. I never have been, and I'm not now, even though you have spoken to me. I get tongue-tied, and my words get tangled'" (Exod. 4:10 NLT). He didn't understand why God would want to use him to do such a mighty task. He didn't feel worthy, and he felt that his skills were lacking in comparison to others. In fact, Moses pleaded with God to send anyone other than him. He didn't doubt God's desire to rescue his people; he just thought God chose the wrong guy.

Like Moses, it's easy to measure and weigh our shortcomings against the directions God calls us to. We're quick to shut him down, believing we aren't worthy enough, especially compared to the next girl. *Thanks, but no thanks, God. Your plans are great, I'm here for the freedom, but I think you have the wrong girl.* What if God had a purpose in asking Moses? I believe he did. What if he has a purpose for you? I believe there is one.

It took some convincing, but with his brother Aaron by his side, Moses did free the Jews from Pharaoh. God had been faithful and had gone before Moses to prepare the way. But what did Moses *do* with all of God's people? Like that awkward moment at an event when the host has run out of things to do and the attendees look around, unsure of how to proceed, Moses needed a plan. After years of glory moments and seeing God's hand through every step, he knew where to turn. That's where we meet him in Exodus 34, seeking God for guidance and wisdom. After each encounter with God, Moses's face glowed with such radiance. Can you imagine? Spending time in the presence of God changes things. It changes you. Moses is proof of this. So, too, are we once we have fully realized our worth and laid that foundation. When we seek the face of God and the truth of his Word, we understand how to shine. That light will then spill out onto everything we do and those around us. This doesn't mean you'll never struggle. Flipping the script may be a lifelong task, and reinforcing the truth consistently is a habit. Like Moses, you can keep going back to the source. Negative thoughts won't dominate your mind and consume your identity once you've learned how to flip the scripts of your life. Your worth has been decided. Now shine like it.

When six months pregnant with my second child, I found myself in a heated game of laser tag. My code name was Big Mama, a name that brought fear to the hearts of many that day. Competitive by nature, I planned to dominate. Still pretty agile, I ran around the course as if winning this game ensured my survival. Nothing would stop my baby and me from making it to the end: I was a modern-day female pregnant Rambo. There was only one problem with my plan; my clothes made it hard for me to hide or sneak up on people. That morning, I forgot to take into account the black lights inside the laser tag room, so my bright white, big baby mama top served as a beacon for unwanted attention and target practice. I couldn't hide no matter how hard I tried. It reminded me of the episode from *Friends* when Ross tries to make a good impression on his blind date by getting his teeth whitened, but he leaves the gel on his teeth way past the allotted time, causing his teeth to glow with brightness. Nervous he may scare off his date, he tries to avoid talking on his date to keep his icy-white teeth hidden. When his date turns off the lights in her apartment, revealing her groovy black light theme, Ross lets down his guard and shows his teeth. To his horror, Ross's teeth illuminate the room like a neon light, thus quickly scaring and ending his date. Yes, I resembled Ross's neon teeth, bobbing and weaving around the crowd of people. Like Ross, I couldn't blend in even if I tried. But even with the glow, I still kicked the tail of my competitors. And to think that I could have wasted all my time trying to hide in the background, not letting anyone see how I shined.

This world is full of darkness, and we can choose to hide, distracted and defeated, feeling overpowered by it all. But if we do this, we forget a fundamental truth written in the book of John: "The light shines in the darkness, and the darkness can never extinguish it" (John 1:5 NLT). The light he speaks of is Christ, and if we follow Jesus, we have that same light inside of us. We are to be the light of the world. We don't run from the dark places; we run to them with the light of Jesus. His Word says this light will never fail or go out. We will shine like Ross's teeth at a disco party in the dark.

One day not long ago, I found myself in a slump. I was just stuck in a rut of comparison, struggles with worth, and feelings of complete failure. A smorgasbord of emotions overwhelmed me and made me want to wave my white flag and crawl back into bed. Denying the sheets that beckoned for me, I attempted something new. The following day, I had a trip booked, and I began to think about how many other people I'd encounter who might resonate with how I felt. What if I could help flip the script for them and make them smile, leaving them better than I found them? And that's when I concocted a plan: creating Bestie Bags.

Never have I ever had so much fun creating those silly little things. Filled with candy, a bestie bracelet, and a card full of confetti *(Are we even surprised by now?)*, the bags were designed to add a bit of joy while I met new people and learned a little about their lives. The cards weren't anything special or extravagant, just a little encouragement reassuring them they were doing a good job and that I was proud of them for showing up today. At the end of the note, I reminded the reader to shine bright, with a reference to Matthew 5:14–16:

> Here's another way to put it: You're here to be light,
> bringing out the God-colors in the world. God is not
> a secret to be kept. We're going public with this, as
> public as a city on a hill. If I make you light-bearers,
> you don't think I'm going to hide you under a bucket,
> do you? I'm putting you on a light stand. Now that
> I've put you there on a hilltop, on a light stand—
> shine! Keep open house; be generous with your lives.
> By opening up to others, you'll prompt people to
> open up with God, this generous Father in heaven.
> (*The Message*)

This is probably one of my favorite verses of all time. How cool to think that we each have the ability to bring out the "God-colors" in this world! We have been crafted to shine in such a way that reflects him and his glory. But we can't hide the light he's given us. Did you see that part? It doesn't make sense to spend time in the Word, learning how to flip our scripts, and begin to shine, only to hide. No, we need to stand tall and shine bright so others can see. They need help, too. They need to see you shining so they understand it's possible, so they have the courage to try, so they know hope is not lost.

Have you ever taken a second to look at a prism? The transparent cut and shaped glass holds a beauty of its own. I have one hanging in my office, and while I enjoy the fun aesthetic it brings to the space, my favorite moment happens when the sunlight hits the prism at the right angle. Because once the light hits the prism, it refracts and shines in other directions. You can often catch a beautiful rainbow glowing across the room—a perfect light of blues, reds, and yellows, God-colors shining for all to see. It's mesmerizing. The light can't stop from shining and refracting off the prism, and with an instant, it becomes involuntary. You are like this prism when you work to fix the damaging scripts taking hold of your life and allow the light of Christ to change you. Soon, his light shining in you begins to refract off of you, and you can't help but create the most incredible God-colors for all to see. You become mesmerizing because you allow God's light to shine. It's not your light; it's his light shining within you. This is the light others need to see.

Two years from my March 2020 flight, I found myself sitting in a buzzing airport with people racing in all directions. People watching is one of my favorite things to do. Tell me I'm not alone. One lady with a leopard-print backpack rushed through the crowd with her hair and clothing threatening to fly off in the opposite direction. This woman was on a mission. Instantly, I was curious. Was she late for her flight? Maybe she needed to use the restroom? Where was she heading? I wondered if it was off on an adventure to an exotic location. With each hurried step, she came that much closer to her escape, leaving all the troubles of her busy life at home. Maybe this was her trek home from a long business trip? What if her journey was to lead to the funeral of someone dear to her?

That's the thing about watching people walk through life—you have no clue where they are going, what are they running from, or how they deal with it all. For me, sitting in the hard blue pleather seats that squeak with every movement (*No, lady—I didn't just pass gas, thank you very much*), next to the window full of dark clouds and rain, people watching has become my own escape. What was I escaping? The idea of my destination. Because I was the girl heading to the funeral of someone dear to me. That's not exactly how I planned to spend my week and, yet, there I was, trying to come to terms with the loss of my grandfather—a man who knew how to incite laughter in a crowd, who knew how to capture the perfect moment through his camera lens, and loved his family dearly. It was all too sad to bear, so I lost myself in watching the crowd.

Each time I get lost in the chaos, imagining the pasts and futures of people who walk by, I'll occasionally catch the eyes of one of them. Without thinking, my mouth quickly shifts to a smile that warms my entire face. Almost instantly, my involuntary reaction is mirrored on their face. We have a moment. It's brief but beautiful. Each of us feels seen in just a smile. This gesture, ever so simple, lifts my spirit and causes me to forget the troubles plaguing my mind. It's a little ray of sun shining through and breaking up a cloudy day. I'd like to think this emotional effect is true for the stranger as well, that they head off to their destination a little lighter and a little brighter.

How can one look alter your mood and change your day? Because your light, even if through just a smile, has power. Your light shines and causes darkness to shatter. Through the work of the Holy Spirit, you have been gifted with this light.

The more you embrace his light and allow it to shine through, the more the effort becomes involuntary, like my smile to a stranger. Even the tiniest of actions can break through the dark spaces in someone's heart and let a little hope in. A smile can bring hope and light to someone. Try it.

Throughout this entire book, I've given you scripts to assist you in flipping from the old negative scripts to new statements of truth found in the Bible. Now I want to give you statements to remind you to shine. We're going to call them Shine Scripts, simple reminders to shine. You're lucky—I came close to calling them Sparkle and Shine Scripts, but I figured not everyone is as extra as I am. Girl, I am guacamole-at-Chipotle extra, and if you don't know of the wonder that is Chipotle, first of all, I am so sorry, you have been wronged, and second, that is an extreme amount of extra. So for your sake, we'll go with Shine Scripts.

- **Shine Script:** *The glory of the Lord shines on me so I can rise and shine* (Isa. 60:1–2).
- **Shine Script:** *I was created to shine brightly for others to see* (Matt. 5:15–16).
- **Shine Script:** *When I share the hope and love of Jesus, I shine like the stars in the sky* (Dan. 12:3).
- **Shine Script:** *The light of Christ is in me and helping me shine and producing what is good, right, and true* (Eph. 5:8–9).

Everything you read in the Bible is yours for the taking. Here's the deal: some of us choose just to read it, and some of us choose to believe it. Don't just read these words; they are yours for the taking. Believe the truth they hold, and let these words change you. Now is the time for you to shine, free and clear from the damaging scripts. Let me implore you as Paul did to the body of believers in Ephesus. Both of you faced a crossroads. Will you allow darkness to come in and affect how you live, breathe, and, ultimately, shine? Will you be persuaded in the ways of culture and the world, or will you remember the truth of God's Word? So I say to you, "Awake, O sleeper, rise up from the dead, and Christ will give you light" (Eph. 5:14 NLT).

Bestie, rise and shine.

CHAPTER 12

Help Flip
THEIR SCRIPTS

A few years ago, I hosted a women's event at a church. The night was full of worship, fun, and a plea for women to rediscover their worth in Christ. There was a stack of pipe cleaners for the women to create crowns to wear at each table. It was something simple and fun, but it was a reminder of the fact that they are daughters of the King of Kings. We had a blast, and the women bought into the theme. It's nice to let loose, have a little fun, and relive the dress-up princess days from childhood. We lose that as we grow. Suddenly, life becomes a series of trials, stressors, and breaking points. The joy of play, princesses, and belief in good tend to fade. But that night, women found themselves believing once again.

One beautiful face in the crowd was a girl named Shantel. Her presence commanded attention, and her name echoed the sparkle and sass she possessed. As I passed by her table while she engaged the women around her in a rousing tale, I stopped to meet this firecracker. It didn't take long for me to realize that Shantel is the quintessential life of the party and someone everyone desires to have in their circle, myself included. She is quick to let you know what's on her mind and is eager to fight for those who need it. Everyone needs a Shantel in their lives. We became fast friends as we talked, and I discovered that she taught at a local elementary school. Even more exciting, she started a program at her school, Project Beauty, for the girls in her grade. The more she shared, the more this girl amazed me.

She created Project Beauty for girls to learn how to be girls, grow in their self-confidence, and have a positive mentor to guide them on the right path. Shantel shared with me that she dealt with bullying throughout her school years and that the bullying worsened in high school. Now as a teacher, looking at her young students, she pictured what it would have looked like to have something like Project Beauty in place for her. At the same time, Shantel began hearing her fourth-graders talk about their struggles with their insecurities and even about life-ending thoughts. It broke her heart to hear how young they were while feeling these feelings, and she decided she needed to do something about it. Her goal was simple yet powerful: to make sure those girls felt loved, supported, and empowered to take on anything they may face in life. Her life had been shaped by struggle and hardships with bullying, but she didn't let those harmful moments and damaging scripts rule her life. Instead, Shantel dug deep to see what might have helped her through those years, and then she became that for other girls, girls who struggled in silence but desperately needed someone to come alongside them and show them the way. She found purpose through her pain by channeling her energy to help those girls.

I wanted to be like her when I grew up. What an inspiration; what a powerhouse.

Shantel's face beamed as she spoke of her proudest moments: when two sisters, who initially couldn't stand being around each other, were able to bond and grow in their relationship; and when a parent came up to thank Shantel for teaching her daughter how to advocate for herself not only in the classroom but with others. "This program is my entire heart," she said. What a strong role model speaking life and hope into the lives of these little girls. Shantel fought to help them flip the damaging scripts already playing in their minds, and then she worked to show them how to rewrite the narrative. A generation was getting a fresh start, all because a teacher, once broken, stepped up to make a change.

I love Shantel's story because she didn't wait for someone to give her permission to do this. She didn't seek to make grand plans in hopes of fame, global reach, or anything fancy like that. Do I believe her idea is genius? You bet. But Shantel didn't consume herself with those thoughts. She simply stepped in and offered what she had (experiences, lessons, etc.) in hopes of changing just one life. It would be worth it all to change even one life. Thankfully, she has shaped the lives of many, which is not surprising in the least. Shantel is a world changer, and I am honored to call her a friend.

It's one thing to live a life of freedom, but it's another to lead people to the same freedom. Did you know suicide is the second leading cause of death in fifteen- to twenty-four-year-olds?[1] And it's in the top ten for those twenty-five and up.[2] Bestie, this statistic is staggering, and the truth is, the problem is only getting worse.[3] We have the opportunity to do something about this, to reframe the narrative of our culture and this generation. Right now, you have the power through the Holy Spirit to help bring change. You can make a difference in the lives around you just like Shantel did. Help them flip their scripts and find hope. This world is desperate for it.

In the Bible, we read about four friends who were desperate for their friend to receive help. What troubled the friend? He was paralyzed. These friends heard of a man named Jesus and of miracles he performed. Full of faith, they carried their friend to a home in Capernaum where Jesus taught. But when they arrived, the four friends were faced with a problem. "They couldn't bring him to Jesus because of the crowd, so they dug a hole through the roof above his head. Then they lowered the man on his mat, right down in front of Jesus. Seeing their faith, Jesus said to the paralyzed man, 'My child, your sins are forgiven'" (Mark 2:4–5 NLT). Nothing would stop these men from bringing their friend to Jesus. Their passion and faith compelled Jesus to speak. Through the power of words, his words, we see what happens next: "Then Jesus turned to the paralyzed man and said, 'Stand up, pick up your mat, and go home!' And the man jumped up, grabbed his mat, and walked out through the stunned onlookers. They were all amazed and praised God, exclaiming, 'We've never seen anything like this before!'" (Mark 2:10–12 NLT). These men didn't struggle to walk, and they were free to move around. But that freedom didn't satisfy them; they dreamed of the same freedom for their friend. Will we have faith like that for our people? Enough faith to show them the way, bring them to Jesus, and help them flip their scripts? Can we be like these men who stopped looking at themselves and saw the needs of others? Their freedom is counting on it.

In sharing this story from Mark, I skimmed over a few verses in the middle. Let's get back to that. After Jesus saw the man lying on the floor in front of him, he said, "My child, your sins are forgiven" (Mark 2:5 NLT). I wonder about the reaction of the onlookers. Did they understand what Jesus spoke? Did they mock or question the presence of this lame man disrupting the room? Was his desperation laughable to them? I'm not sure, but in my experience, not everyone will be excited for you. Not everyone will understand. Often, through that lack of understanding or spite, they will speak words that tear you down. In this case, we see a glimpse of the reactions in the following verse:

> But some of the teachers of religious law who were sitting there thought to themselves, "What is he saying? This is blasphemy! Only God can forgive sins!"
> Jesus knew immediately what they were thinking, so he asked them, "Why do you question this in your hearts? Is it easier to say to the paralyzed man 'Your sins are forgiven,' or 'Stand up, pick up your mat, and walk'? So I will prove to you that the Son of Man has the authority on earth to forgive sins."
> (Mark 2:6–10 NLT)

What if the paralyzed man had listened to the questioning of the crowd or the Pharisees? What if the interaction between them and Jesus had made the paralyzed man nervous? What if he thought that his friends were acting foolishly? Then, filled with humility and fear, this man might have allowed the words of others to create a barrier between him and his healing—between him and his freedom—all from bitter men who lacked understanding. We see it often in Scripture, instances similar to the rantings of Pharisees who acted in fear and spoke bold words that proved untrue and caused damage. Our words and actions hold power—how will you use them? I would be remiss to not point out that doubt, criticism, and even suffering ended at the feet of Jesus. When you fight to flip the script in your mind, whether from words of your own or those of others, they are no match for God's Word. Bring them to the feet of Jesus, and watch him silence the critics and tell you to pick up your mat and walk.

Not long ago, I posted this caption on Instagram: "Sticks and stones can break my bones, but words can really crush me." This was my response to receiving a comment on a previous video from a stranger that said, "Please get off the Internet."

Can I be transparent for a second? Those five little words felt like a bee sting to the heart. Why didn't this stranger like me? Also, why do people troll the Internet desiring to cause trouble? Did my posting warrant the need for me to ban myself from the online space? From the way I viewed the situation, I had two ways of dealing with the comment: reply with a snarky quip, or ignore it. I did neither of these. Instead, I sweetly replied, "I'm sorry you feel this way." My heart struggled with wanting to lash out like this stranger did. But I quickly realized those words wouldn't change things for the better, and they could make the situation worse. Even more so, outsiders looking on could assume my words were just as unkind. All of this angst derived from a comment made by someone hiding behind the safety of their computer.

The Internet is tricky like that. I can say or type out something, and I have no control over how someone perceives it.

Will all caps make them think I am yelling? If they really knew me, they'd understand it was Brittany-sized excitement. They could read it as a joke or even as a threat. One thing I knew, that stranger's comments hurt.

After typing out my response, I threw down my phone and went about my way. What happened next, I did not expect. The stranger left *another* comment. "My apologies, that was harsh but I meant it jokingly . . . my bad." Did he just apologize? A smile shot across my face, not because he apologized, but because I knew there was hope for humanity. You guys, people are good. Do we make mistakes? Yes. Shoot, I've made plenty of them, and my words have cut people deeply. But here's the thing to remember from all this: *you can ask for forgiveness.* There is nothing more beautiful than a human being seeking to honor another person and admit their mistake. That's huge, that's powerful, and that gives hope for the future. Friends, let's be a part of the change and use our words to bring life! Even if we mess up, let's restore the damage we may have caused. Everyone is worthy of that.

A precious Instagram follower named Vera messaged me after I shared my post telling the story of my Internet troll and our interaction online. She told me of the struggle she faced in her mind due to the damaging words spoken over her as a child. From a place of pain, this follower's mom discounted anything she did or strived to succeed in. *You will never amount to anything. You are just like your father.* For a long time, Vera believed those words, and she replayed them in her mind like a painful, catchy slogan running circles. She grew up, and through counseling, great friends, and the help of Jesus, Vera flipped that script. She also added that her life would appear successful to a bystander, but that none of that mattered. Words that used to hold her in bondage were broken by the truth of God's word.

"Brittany, words matter. Man, do they hold the power of life and death." I couldn't have said it any better. When we help others change the scripts they believe, we also need to take stock of the words we've spoken. Do we need to flip them from death to life? Bestie, let's lead the way to others' freedom by being the first to apologize and help them flip the scripts on the things we've said. I never want my words to be the thing holding someone in bondage. I bet the same is true of you.

Can I tell you a secret? Lean in real close. Sometimes you have to be your own hype girl and jump in to be proactive for the moments when remembering truth seems to be difficult. I know this because my husband taught me. Like the friends fighting to bring their struggling pal to the feet of Jesus, he constantly looks for ways to remind me of God's Word. Sam has always held the title of my biggest supporter, and he knows exactly how to keep me moving forward when I feel defeated. Who knew a life coach would be so good at encouraging others and yet struggle to remember things for herself? Well, it's true. *Cue face-palm.*

A few years ago, I sat on the floor in a hotel hallway telling my husband about the crazy revelation God had just given me. "I'm supposed to champion women to freedom!" Never had anything seemed so clear to me, and at that moment, nothing could stop me. A passion burned so deeply in my soul for these women and their freedom. It was an Esther moment, for sure.

But before I could say another word, Sam interrupted me. "Brittany, maybe you should take a second while you're on this high and film a video coaching yourself for the moments you doubt. This process could take a while, and you need to remember what God said to you today." What? I didn't need a video of me talking to myself, but I humored him and filmed one anyway. Can I tell you something? He was right! (Please don't tell him.) There have been many times during this book journey when I've questioned what God spoke to me that day. My memory gets distorted by time, fear, and discouragement. But in those moments, I know where to go: back to my video. That Brittany was unstoppable for the things God had called her to. She didn't know exactly where the path would lead, but she charged forward by boldly believing God. Her unapologetic belief and passion ignite a fire in me all over again each time I watch. These were the words to myself; by now, I can quote them by heart.

> Brittany, I wanted to encourage you tonight as you're sitting here in a hotel, reeling from the few days that you've gotten to spend at this coaching retreat. I wanted to take a second and film this in case at this moment you are questioning what God has said. He has confirmed over and over again that you are meant to speak to women; you are meant to bring them freedom.
>
> So remember the verse, Esther 4:14. Brittany, God has called you for this purpose. And if you don't stand up and do that, he's going to bring someone else along to do it instead. Then you will miss the blessings from it. Who knows, maybe you were created for such a time as this. Remember who you're passionate about and what happens if you don't. So don't be fearful; fight for "her." Okay? Believe it.

Maybe Sam was onto something. Maybe the best thing you can do is to record yourself in the moments when you hear God so clearly, when breakthrough comes and you find yourself shining bright. With this light, you become your own hype girl.

Queen Esther is one of my favorite characters in the Bible. She displayed such wisdom, courage, and strength throughout her life. I love bold aggressive moments of bravery, like William Wallace of real-life and *Braveheart* fame exhibited. We're not surprised by this at all, are we? But sometimes, quiet, feminine strength can be beautiful. Esther's story does this well. At the beginning of the book of Esther, King Xerxes finds himself looking for another queen. Apparently, the last queen embarrassed him during a royal party, and, in his anger, he decided to banish and humiliate her. Yikes. In his search for a new queen, he sent his servants to find the most beautiful and talented women to choose from. Esther found herself among the few, thanks to her wisdom and favor. King Xerxes became smitten with Esther. "And the king loved Esther more than any of the other young women. He was so delighted with her that he set the royal crown on her head and declared her queen" (Esther 2:17 NLT). During her reign as queen, her cousin Mordecai rose in status, enabling him to work near her at the castle. Through his wisdom, he warned Esther before she became queen to keep quiet about her nationality and their relation to one another. When Mordecai angered Haman, a prideful leader and righthand man to the king, by refusing to bow to him, a plot was crafted to annihilate him and the Jewish people. Esther feared for her life as well as for the lives of her people. How could their fate be spared? But even through the deceit and threats brought on by Haman, Esther showed wisdom and strength. She leaned on the truth and guidance of those she trusted, those who helped keep her mind and heart at peace.

As the threat of death neared, Mordecai implored Esther to rise up and fight for the Jewish people, her people. "For if you remain silent at this time, relief and deliverance for the Jews will arise from another place, but you and your father's family will perish. And who knows but that you have come to your royal position for such a time as this?" (Esther 4:14 NIV). Esther had a choice. Would she give way to the fear and the negative scripts in her mind? Or would she listen to her cousin? He had a plan to help her. He knew God would protect her, and he knew she wouldn't be alone. Her choice would free a generation of people or lead to their massacre. As scary as it all seemed, the power was in her hands. Mordecai wanted her to see that God had positioned her for just this time and that he could be trusted with their futures. Mordecai knew the truth and fought to help Esther to see it. What if your role in helping others flip their scripts could impact a generation? What if you could be the Mordecai to someone's Esther? What if you hold the power, through what you've learned, to take part in helping someone else shape and change the world? Spoiler alert: you do, and you can.

Let me be Mordecai to you for a second. I took the well-known verse in chapter 4 of Esther and adapted it a little to help you. This is my attempt to call you into action, just as Mordecai did to Esther. While you probably aren't freeing the Jewish people from imminent death, you can help bring freedom from harmful thought patterns that can be just as damaging. I want to invite you into this script. Let's call it a little charge or encouragement over you as you help others fight for their freedom. For me, it helps to write down statements or verses that I want to remember on cards and stick them in places I pass by throughout my day. I'd like to encourage you to do the same.

(Your Name Here), God has called you to rise up and help a generation flip their scripts. And if you don't stand up and do that, he's going to bring someone else along to do it instead. Then you will miss the blessings from it. Who knows? Maybe you were created for such a time as this.

Look around you. Who else needs this message? Other women in your life are watching you and looking to you for help, consciously or not. Inevitably, helping others is what this book has been about: to help set other women free, to help them shine and rewrite their stories. Women everywhere are missing out on abundant life and are underutilizing their God-given gifts because they've given into these negative scripts. They are drowning, and they're looking for help. You have done the work of flipping your script; now train others to do the same. I don't want to do this alone—can we do it together?

Let me leave you with this challenge. Pray, and ask God to show you a friend who needs this message. Maybe it's a coworker you see every day, the neighbor you wave to as you check the mail, or a family member whom you know the deep struggles of their heart. When this person comes to mind, I challenge you to give them a copy of this book. Nothing fancy or extreme needs to happen. Just tell them you've read this book and wanted to pass it along as encouragement. Bonus points if you add that you'll be praying for them as they read through it. Here's the kicker: offer to be there if they have questions. (P.S. I'm here, too. Call or text me—my number is in the back of this book.)

You can help flip their scripts. Who knows? Maybe you were created for such a time as this!

Notes

[1] Sandy Cohen, "Suicide Rate Highest among Teens and Young Adults," UCLA Health, March 15, 2022, https://connect.uclahealth.org/2022/03/15 /suicide-rate-highest-among-teens-and-young-adults/.

[2] National Institute of Mental Health, "Suicide," accessed September 15, 2022, https://www.nimh.nih.gov/health/statistics/suicide.

[3] Suicide Prevention Resource Center, "Suicide By Age," accessed September 15, 2022, https://sprc.org/scope/age.

Benediction:

FLIP YOUR SCRIPT

At thirty-seven weeks pregnant, I became accustomed to a constant state of discomfort. Adding an extra layer of complexity was my eighteen-month-old daughter glued to my chest, crying and sick. Why do sick kids just want their mom? Daddy won't do; they need their mama. Bless it. I was both equally annoyed and flattered at the same time. At that moment, tired doesn't even begin to describe the state I was in. My daughter's decline started out as a simple fever. With three little kids, Sam and I weren't worried, and we assumed she just had a virus that needed to pass. No big deal. Like clockwork, we gave her the designated meds to break her fever and relieve her pain. Still, she cried. She soothed when we rocked her, so that's what we did. After a serious round of bribery and nego-tiations, Sam took over, allowing me to have a break. Never underestimate the power of a sick baby; they are stern, stubborn, and not easy to persuade at all.

Freedom! Finally, I had a moment to myself, and, like any respectable pregnant woman, I marched into the kitchen for a snack. I deserved a reward for surviving the mayhem of the morning. Toddlers aren't much different from pregnant women. They are both stubborn, whiny, and hungry. Only a few blissful moments into my reprieve, Sam yelled out for me. Normally, I would shrug it off, maybe yell back to see what he needed, or possibly pretend to not hear him, because he did just take over. *Give it a chance, Sam, give it a chance.* But something in his voice sounded different; it sounded urgent and panicked. The next few minutes were a blur. "Brittany, I need you now! Somethings wrong; I don't know what's happening. What do we do?" His words still echo in my mind to this day. My snack crashed to the floor as I darted down the hall to see my baby. Sam pulled our daughter away from his chest. She didn't cry, and she didn't move. "I think she is having a seizure. She's burning up, we need to cool her off."

We locked eyes, and without any words spoken, we both understood the great desperation and fear gripping us. We carefully laid her on the ground as I called out for my baby to answer. "Paisley, Paisley, can you hear mommy?" She was there; I knew she was. Could she just answer her mommy? Her eyes were cold, blank, and lifeless, and my heart was being ripped in two. Those once feverish rosy cheeks had turned shades of blue and purple. How I hated those colors. If only her lips could call out for me, let me know she could hear, but they didn't. My girl, my little girl, lay on the floor struggling and twitching as I sat helplessly next to her body. What were we to do? I had no clue; I was not prepared.

"Come back. PLEASE! It's okay, baby. It's okay. I love you." Sobbing uncontrollably, I gasped for air. Why didn't I know what to do? They have books labeled "What to Expect When . . . " that cover all the topics you can imagine, but not this one. Nobody ever tells you what to expect when your child has a seizure. My face burned with fury. We could lose our baby girl, and I sat unprepared to stop it. Seconds seemed like hours, and minutes seemed like a lifetime. *Why did time move so slow?*

Just then, I started to notice different movements from my girl. She began to cry and looked up at me. She looked at me! In shock and disbelief, tears flowed down my cheeks as I thanked the Lord that my baby was still alive. Could I grab her? I had no idea of the protocol. My heart ached to scoop her up, hold her close, and never let her go. She cried, and she needed me. I would give my life for this girl. After a crazy interaction with 911, Sam hung up the phone and furiously ran through the house gathering toys, diaper bags, and ice packs. Since the ambulance couldn't make it to us, we'd take matters into our own hands and race to the hospital ourselves. Sam maneuvered the streets with skills that rivaled NASCAR drivers. I held our girl in my arms, fearful she might seize again. "It's okay, baby. Just stay awake for mommy. Please stay awake." She cried the entire ride to the hospital.

The boys, in the back row, yelled for each other to plug their ears. "She's crying so loud. Mom, make her stop!" You've got to love toddlers—they had no idea what was going on, but they were annoyed by her screams. The swirl of chaos around me brought on bursts of tearful laughter. My baby cried, the boys fought, and, for a split second, things seemed normal.

Our frantic arrival to the hospital was met with hours of uncertainty as we waited for answers. They ran test after test, and all signs pointed to febrile seizures. In case you have no clue what this means, like I didn't, these seizures are most common in children. They can be triggered when a child's fever spikes or drops rapidly, and, thankfully, they are usually not harmful. Each doctor or nurse we encountered assured us that these seizures are common in children, and while these words were spoken to bring comfort, they only angered me. How could they be so common if I knew nothing about them? Three children in, and it took a traumatic event for me to hear this term? Their nonchalant nature made me feel foolish for my sense of panic. Normal or not, it felt monumental to me.

There's confidence that comes when you're prepared. I lacked the confidence in my skills as a mother, in protecting my daughter, because I wasn't prepared. If I had known what to do, I would have done it. But I had been thrown a curveball and didn't know how to swing. Instead of hitting a home run, I stood there feeling angry and unequipped, ultimately feeling like I struck out. I just needed someone to teach me and show me the way.

Watching the Olympics is one of our favorite things to do as a family. We might be a little obsessed, obsessed to the point of creating our own Estes Olympics. Our house gets an Olympic-themed makeover, we create events for our family to compete in, and we crown the winners with medals. It's incredible and intense, but that's how we roll in the Estes household. As we sit on the couch cheering for the athletes as they compete, we can't help but notice a common theme with their demeanor. They carry themselves with confidence. Some are a little cockier than others, but each athlete appears honored to represent their country and compete. Why are they confident? Because they have prepared for the event. It wasn't a spur-of-the-moment decision that led to anxiety over their performance abilities. No, they spent hours, months, and years training and preparing for their event. Their preparation led to their confidence.

My desire is for you to have confidence, too. Unlike how I felt with my daughter and her seizure, I want you to be prepared. Negative scripts may be a common practice in your mind. That's okay. But while these scripts can be scary and damaging, you can confidently change them. That's why I wrote this book. It's time for you to train and prepare, to use this guide for what to do when you feel those scripts try to creep in. You aren't unprepared and helpless. No, you are equipped and ready.

Days may come when you struggle to remember what you've learned, and that's okay. Pick up this book, and check back in with the "flip the script" sections. It's work, it takes practice, but, like Nehemiah yelled out to his enemies as they tried to distract and taunt him ("I am doing a great work and I cannot come down. Why should the work stop while I leave it and come down to you?" [Neh. 6:3 ESV]), you, bestie, are doing good work, the work that brings freedom, breaks chains, and changes lives. Don't get distracted, and don't stop. Build confidence as you continue the work.

Okay, if I haven't shocked you enough in this book, try this on for size. In my senior year of high school, I decided to compete in the school's beauty pageant. The pageant was more of a glorified popularity contest, where model-worthy beautiful girls sang and pranced around for all to see. That sounded like a fun opportunity for the average girl whose singing made dogs howl. I could have a little fun and shake things up. Did I want to win the competition? Of course. But first and foremost, I desired to have fun and make new friends. They asked questions like, "What is your favorite food?" Macaroni and cheese: solid answer. I sauntered across the stage in my bubblegum-pink dress adorned with thousands of crystals, with my hunky tux-wearing boyfriend by my side. Spoiler alert: that boyfriend is now my hunky husband. Well-played, high school Brittany; well-played.

When the time came for the talent portion, I did the only thing I knew to do: storytelling. My high school years were spent on a competitive acting team where my signature event had always been storytelling. The idea behind the event was to make a children's book come to life. I created locations and scenes, and I embodied each character to tell my story. My only prop was a single chair. Nothing brought me joy like storytelling did. So that night, I took the stage, explained to the audience the greatness they were about to behold, and put on a show. This particular book involved me on all fours mooing like a constipated cow—real glamorous pageant material right there! One of the other characters was a magical genie who piped up with his trademark line each time he granted a wish. I'd strike a pose, with a finger pointed to the sky while I channeled my best disco vibes, and yell something along the lines of, "I've got the power!" at the top of my lungs. The crowd, which was witnessing something never done on the pageant stage, roared with laughter. In the shock of a lifetime, I won the pageant that year. Shoot, I swept the entire event—I won Miss Congeniality and tied for Best Talent. Who would have ever thought? A girl who decided to play the game the only way she knew how, as fully herself, won.

Take a lesson from high school Brittany. The best person to be is yourself. Play the game the only way you know how to, the way God created you to. But even more than that, I want you to know that you have the power. You have the power to flip the script and reframe the narrative of your mind. If you need a laugh or little reminder to keep trying, just picture me singing this over you: *You've got the power!* Or you can call me and I'll do it. Your girl isn't afraid; I just believe in you that much.

Closing out this book proved a challenge for me. Do I send you off with a declaration, cheer you on as a friend, or coach you like I would a client? All angles to wrap this sucker up are available and valid, but none of them settled well until one afternoon when I sat at the computer in my office, plagued by writer's block. This happens when you spend hours in front of a computer screen and hope to continually spit out *magic*. But through this whole process, the Lord has been so gracious and filled me with inspiration and words when I needed them most. So the idea of staring at a blank screen, though daunting at the moment, needed a little "flip the script" in my heart. Alexa came in clutch by playing worship music, and I began to pray for you, the reader, as I often do. A few songs into the mix, "The Blessing" by Kari Jobe, Cody Carnes, and Elevation Worship began to play. Tears streamed down my face as I cried out to God on your behalf. I motioned over the computer screen for the Lord to show you favor, to bring you freedom, and for it to trickle down from your generation and to the next generation and so on. I wanted his presence to go before you and beside you, for him to be all around you as you work to reframe the narrative in your mind and allow God's truth to saturate it completely.

Until this moment, the weight of these words—God's words for you, which have been burdening my heart—haven't fully been expressible. This is freedom for your generation, for the ones behind you, and for those who follow. It's something we've laughed together about, cried over, and, hopefully, has caused us to mark up the pages of this book. One truth remains. Through the power of Christ in you, you have the ability to flip your script. My heart beats for you to fully comprehend this freedom, but God desires it even more.

If you were to come over to my house, have a meal, and maybe some coffee, we'd inevitably get to the heart. Don't get me wrong: I'm a party girl and am always up for a good laugh, but that can only take us so far. If we're going to be friends, I want to know your heart. This book was our living room coffee chat. Maybe one day, we can do it in person for real. Can we be besties? But until then, I hope you've felt the love of a bestie walking alongside you and cheering you on like a Dallas Cowboys Cheerleader. That's a lot of cheer, in case you didn't know.

If we had our heart talk in the comfort of my home, there would be a point at which you'd need to leave. You know, because of families and lives and everything in between. I'm sad about it too. We would hug, and I'd probably snap a picture to post on "the Gram" (aka Instagram). But before you headed out, your eyes would catch a glimpse of something sparkly and fantastic displayed above my front door: an incredible painting my sweet friend made for me and probably one of my favorite things hanging in my home. Full of brilliant jewel-toned colors with highlights of gold, it boasts words that are near and dear to my heart. Written in the most beautifully playful script (because, you know, who would want it any other way?), it's sure to melt your heart and bring a smile to your face with just one glance. Why does it hang above my door? Because I desire for everyone leaving my home to have this blessing imparted to them. It's like sending you off with a love note from Jesus and me. And I love every bit of it.

Since our time is up, the coffee cups are dry, and you're about to leave, here's my blessing over you from that painting as you shut this book and take on this world. It's a little love note from Jesus and me:

The LORD bless you
    and keep you;
the LORD make his face shine on you
    and be gracious to you;
the LORD turn his face toward you
    and give you peace. (Num. 6:24–26 NIV)

Go out and flip the script.

ACKNOWLEDGMENTS

Sam—nobody on this earth has ever believed in me as much as you do. You remind me of the calling God has given me and won't let me settle for anything less. I know that I often discredit the praise you shower me with, but I'm incredibly grateful to have a best friend and husband like you. You are my biggest fan, and I am yours. Thank you for being on my team forever. You're my lobster.

My kids (Ethan, James, Poppy, Titus, Paisley, Penelope, and Pippa)—you are the coolest bunch of kids a mom could ask for. I love all your unique qualities and cannot wait to watch you change this world. You are the greatest calling I'll ever have. Thank you for understanding when I needed to hide away writing for hours, for cheering me on every step of the way, and for telling me you're proud of me. I will never forget any of that.

Family—without your love and support I wouldn't be the woman, wife, or mother I am today. Mom, Dad, Shawnda, and Stephanie, thank you for cheering me on, pushing me further, and letting this crazy girl be who God made her to be. I love you all and am so thankful to call you my family!

To my bowl girls, Jessica and Jolynne—we have done a lot of life together. It's been full of ups and downs, but there isn't a pair I would rather go through it with. You are my sisters. Thank you for showing me what true, deep friendship looks like. You have held my arms up through some of the toughest days, including writing this book, and I hope to be even half the friend you are to me. Ecclesiastes 4:12.

Heather—you, my friend, deserve a gold medal in dealing with all my ups and downs during this process. Every time, though, you were so faithful to point me back to Jesus and the reason I began this journey. Thank you for praying, challenging, and celebrating with me.

Jess Connolly—remember back in the day when we were tired moms on Twitter looking for connection and believing we had influence right where our feet were planted? I'm so thankful God allowed for our paths to cross. You have championed me for years, and this book is a shining example of that. *Thank you* cannot even begin to tell you how I feel. Thank you for using your gifts, influence, and passion for others. The ripple effect of your life is enormous and will be seen for generations to come.

GATG coaches/team—GIRLS!!!! You are a sisterhood like none other. I am thankful for your coaching and cheering. I'm so glad we get to do this together. I'm on your team forever.

Michele—do you remember the day you gave me the most precious card with a girl in a pink floral dress? It was over brunch at our favorite spot and the words inside have stuck with me all these years later: "I believe in you so much, and believe that when you are ready, the world needs to hear your story!" The card is displayed in my office, and I look to it often because it makes me feel like you are in the room with me. I could never adequately tell you how much your friendship means to me, but I hope you somehow know. Thank you for being who you are.

Liz—you took all my jumbled ideas, passionate talks, and mess, and turned them into something beautiful. Thank you for encouraging me, showing me the ropes, and pushing me as a writer. A lot of life happened during the making of this project, and I consider it an honor to have been able to pray for you through it. The biggest blessing: sweet baby Fiona and her life! This book was my baby and you helped birth her with me. You were my coach.

Mary—thank you for believing in a feisty, pink-haired underdog. I'm thankful that you saw my heart and passion and believed in my message more than the size of my following.

Jason, Duane, Mary, and the Leafwood team—never during this process have I taken for granted your willingness to champion this message. It's a dream, and you have helped bring it to life. I will forever be grateful to you, and I pray the Lord will help you see the harvest that comes from this project and your faithfulness. Thank you, thank you, thank you.

Connect with Brittany

Brittany is passionate about people. She wants everyone to be a "Bestie" and would love to hear from you if you want to email her at jbrittanyestes@gmail.com. You can continue the fun by following her on Instagram, Twitter, and Facebook, @jbrittanyestes.

Like she said in her book, here's her cell phone number if you want to give her a call: (601) 706-9851.

Brittany is a life coach. She specializes in helping women find breakthrough, purpose, and direction in their lives. If you're interested booking a session with her, you can find out more at brittanyestes.com/coaching. She is also available to inspire and engage your church, team, or audience. Brittany is a dynamic speaker who has spoken all across the country, bringing her unique perspective and exciting storytelling with her. If you're interested in having Brittany come to your next event, check out brittanyestes.com/speak.